Rick Steves®

POCKET
ROME

Rick Steves & Gene Openshaw

Contents

Introduction 3

Heart of Rome Walk 15

Colosseum Tour 25

Roman Forum Tour 39

St. Peter's Basilica Tour 55

Vatican Museums Tour 79

Borghese Gallery Tour 109

Sights 125

Activities 167

Sleeping 175

Eating 183

Practicalities 197

Index 213

Introduction

Rome is magnificent and overwhelming at the same time. It's a showcase of Western civilization, with astonishingly ancient sights and a modern vibrancy. But with the wrong attitude, you'll be frustrated by the kind of chaos that only an Italian can understand. On a previous visit, a cabbie struggling with the traffic said, *"Roma chaos."* I responded, *"Bella chaos."* He agreed.

Two thousand years ago the word "Rome" meant civilization itself. Everything was either civilized (part of the Roman world) or barbarian. Today, Rome is Italy's political capital, the heart of Catholicism, and the center of its ancient empire, littered with evocative remains. As you peel through the city's fascinating layers, you'll find Rome's monuments, cats, laundry, cafés, churches, fountains, traffic, and 2.8 million people endlessly entertaining.

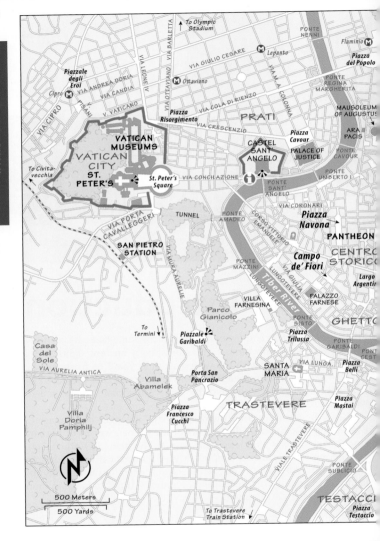

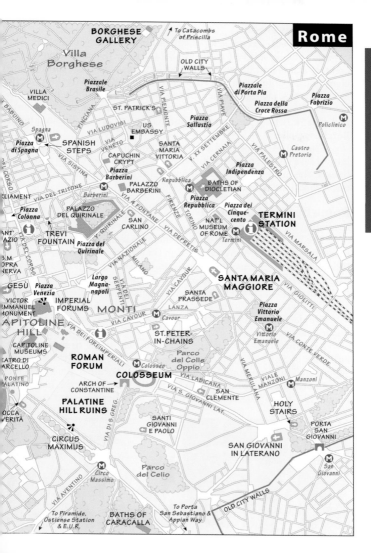

About This Book

Rick Steves Pocket Rome is a personal tour guide...in your pocket. The core of the book is six self-guided walks and tours that zero in on Rome's greatest sights and experiences. Do the "Caesar shuffle" through ancient Rome's Colosseum and Forum. Stroll from Campo de' Fiori to the Spanish Steps, lacing together Rome's Baroque and bubbly nightspots. Learn something about eternity by touring the huge Vatican Museums, and visit St. Peter's, the greatest church on earth. Savor the sumptuous Borghese Gallery.

The rest of this book is a traveler's tool kit, with my best advice on how to save money, plan your time, use public transportation, and avoid lines at the busiest sights. You'll also get recommendations on hotels, restaurants, and activities.

Rome by Neighborhood

Sprawling Rome actually feels manageable once you get to know it.

The historic core, with most of the tourist sights, sits inside a diamond formed by Termini train station (in the east), the Vatican (west), Villa Borghese Gardens (north), and the Colosseum (south). The Tiber River snakes through the diamond from north to south. At the center of the diamond is Piazza Venezia, a busy square and traffic hub. It takes about an hour to walk from Termini train station to Vatican City.

Think of Rome as a collection of neighborhoods, huddling around major landmarks.

Ancient Rome: In ancient times, this was home to the grandest buildings of a city of a million people. Today, the best of the classical sights stand in a line from the Colosseum to the Forum to the Pantheon.

Pantheon Neighborhood: The Pantheon anchors the neighborhood I like to call the Heart of Rome. It stretches eastward from the

Rome's Neighborhoods

Tiber River through Campo de' Fiori and Piazza Navona, past the Pantheon to the Trevi Fountain.

Vatican City: Located west of the Tiber, this a compact world of its own, with two great, massive sights: St. Peter's Basilica and the Vatican Museums.

North Rome: With the Spanish Steps, Borghese Gallery, Villa Borghese Gardens, and trendy shopping streets (Via Veneto and the "shopping triangle"), this is a more modern, classy area.

East Rome: This neighborhood around Termini Station boasts the stunning National Museum of Rome and many recommended hotels and public-transportation connections. To the south and east is the area I call Pilgrim's Rome, with several prominent churches.

Rome at a Glance

▲▲▲**Colosseum** Huge stadium where gladiators fought. **Hours:** Daily 9:00 until one hour before sunset: April-Aug until 19:15, Sept until 19:00, Oct until 18:30, off-season closes as early as 16:30. See page 126.

▲▲▲**Roman Forum** Ancient Rome's main square, with ruins and grand arches. **Hours:** Same hours as Colosseum. See page 126.

▲▲▲**Capitoline Museums** Ancient statues, mosaics, and expansive view of the Forum. **Hours:** Daily 9:30-19:30. See page 131.

▲▲▲**Pantheon** The defining domed temple. **Hours:** Daily 9:00-19:00, closed for Mass Sat at 17:00 and Sun at 10:30. See page 138.

▲▲▲**St. Peter's Basilica** Most impressive church on earth, with Michelangelo's *Pietà* and dome. **Hours:** Church—daily 7:00-19:00, Oct-March until 18:30, often closed Wed mornings; dome—daily 7:00-17:00. See page 143.

▲▲▲**Vatican Museums** Four miles of the finest art of Western civilization, culminating in Michelangelo's glorious Sistine Chapel. **Hours:** Mon-Sat 9:00-18:00 (Fri-Sat until 22:30 in late April-Oct), closed Sun—except last Sun of month, when it's open 9:00-14:00. See page 143.

▲▲▲**Borghese Gallery** Bernini sculptures and paintings by Caravaggio, Raphael, and Titian in a Baroque palazzo. **Hours:** Tue-Sun 9:00-19:00, closed Mon. See page 145.

▲▲▲**National Museum of Rome** Greatest collection of Roman sculpture anywhere. **Hours:** Tue-Sun 9:00-19:45, closed Mon. See page 149.

▲▲**Trajan's Column, Market, and Forum** Tall column with narrative relief, forum ruins, and museum with entry to Trajan's Market. **Hours:** Forum and column always viewable; museum open daily 9:30-19:30. See page 135.

▲▲**St. Peter-in-Chains** Church with Michelangelo's *Moses*. **Hours:** Daily 7:15-12:30 & 15:00-19:00, Oct-March until 18:00. See page 137.

▲▲**Museo dell'Ara Pacis** Shrine marking the beginning of Rome's Golden Age. **Hours:** Daily 9:30-19:30. See page 148.

▲▲**Dolce Vita Stroll** Evening *passeggiata*, where Romans strut their stuff. **Hours:** Roughly Mon-Sat 17:00-19:00 and Sun afternoons. See page 147.

▲▲**Catacombs** Underground tombs, mainly Christian, some outside the city. **Hours:** Generally 10:00-12:00 & 14:00-17:00. See pages 149 and 158.

▲▲**Church of San Giovanni in Laterano** Grandiose and historic "home church of the popes," with one-of-a-kind Holy Stairs across the street. **Hours:** Daily 7:00-18:30. See page 153.

▲**Palatine Hill** Ruins of emperors' palaces, Circus Maximus view, and museum. **Hours:** Same hours as Colosseum. See page 128.

▲**Mamertine Prison** Ancient prison where Saints Peter and Paul were held. **Hours:** Daily 9:00-17:00, may stay open later in summer. See page 132.

▲**Arch of Constantine** Honors the emperor who legalized Christianity. See page 126.

▲**The Roman House at Palazzo Valentini** Remains of an ancient house and bath. **Hours:** Wed-Mon 10:00-19:00, closed Tue, may have shorter hours off-season. See page 136.

▲**Piazza del Campidoglio** Square atop Capitoline Hill, designed by Michelangelo, with a museum, grand stairway, and Forum overlooks. See page 131.

▲**Victor Emmanuel Monument** Gigantic edifice celebrating Italian unity, with Rome from the Sky elevator ride up to 360-degree city view. **Hours:** Daily 9:30-19:30. See page 133.

▲**Trevi Fountain** Baroque hot spot into which tourists throw coins to ensure a return trip to Rome. See page 142.

▲**Castel Sant'Angelo** Hadrian's Tomb turned castle, prison, papal refuge, and now museum. **Hours:** Tue-Sun 9:00-19:30, closed Mon. See page 144.

▲**Baths of Diocletian/Basilica S. Maria degli Angeli** Once ancient Rome's immense public baths, now a Michelangelo church. **Hours:** Mon-Sat 10:00-13:00 & 16:00-18:30, Sun until 19:00, may be open mid-day in summer. See page 151.

Trastevere: This colorful, wrong-side-of-the-river neighborhood has a village feel. South of Vatican City and just west of the Pantheon neighborhood, it's the city at its crustiest—and perhaps most "Roman."

South Rome: Here are the funky Testaccio neighborhood, the 1930s suburb of E.U.R., and the Appian Way, home of the catacombs.

Planning Your Time

The following day plans give an idea of how much an organized, motivated, and caffeinated person can see.

You won't be able to see everything, so don't try. Budget time for Rome after dark. Dine well at least once.

Day 1: Do the "Caesar Shuffle" from the Colosseum to the Roman Forum and Palatine Hill, and on to the Pantheon. After a siesta, add some sightseeing to suit your interest. In the evening enjoy a sound-and-light show at the Forum and/or a colorful stroll in Trastevere or the Monti district.

Day 2: See Vatican City (St. Peter's, dome climb, Vatican Museums). Have dinner near the atmospheric Campo de' Fiori, and then walk to the Trevi Fountain and Spanish Steps (following my "Heart of Rome Walk").

Day 3: Visit the Borghese Gallery and the Capitoline Museums. In the evening, join the locals in the Dolce Vita Stroll *passeggiata*.

With More Time: Choose from other major sights: National Museum of Rome, the catacombs, Museo dell'Ara Pacis, Trajan's Column, the churches of Pilgrim's Rome—or peruse the Sights chapter for more options. Explore a local street market, stroll through the Villa Borghese Gardens, or take a side trip to Ostia Antica or Tivoli.

When to Go

Rome's best travel months (also its busiest and most expensive) are April, May, June, September, October, and early November. These months combine the convenience of peak season with pleasant weather.

The most grueling thing about travel in Rome is the summer heat in July and August, when temperatures can soar to the high 90s and pricier hotels discount their rooms. Air-conditioning is the norm in all but the cheapest hotels (though it's generally available only from June through September). Spring and fall can be cool, and many hotels do not turn on their heat.

Rome is fine in winter—cool and crisp with temperatures in the 40s and 50s. Street life stays in full swing all year, as restaurants set up heaters

🎧 Rick's Free Video Clips and Audio Tours

Rick Steves Classroom Europe, a powerful tool for teachers, is also useful for travelers. This video library contains about 500 short clips excerpted from my public television series. Enjoy these videos as you sort through options for your trip and to better understand what you'll see in Europe. Check it out at Classroom.RickSteves.com (just enter a topic to find everything I've filmed on a subject).

   Rick Steves Audio Europe, a free app, makes it easy to download my audio tours and listen to them offline as you travel. For this book (look for the 🎧), these audio tours include my Heart of Rome and Trastevere walks plus tours of the Pantheon, St. Peter's Basilica, Roman Forum, Colosseum, Sistine Chapel, Vatican Museums, and Ostia Antica. The app also offers interviews (organized by country) from my public radio show with experts from Europe and around the globe. Find it in your app store or at RickSteves.com/AudioEurope.

to warm outdoor tables, and nativity scenes grace churches through January. Off-season has none of the sweat and stress of the tourist season, but sights may have shorter hours, lunchtime breaks, and fewer activities. Confirm your sightseeing plans locally, especially when traveling off-season.

Before You Go

You'll have a smoother trip if you tackle a few things ahead of time. For more details on these topics, see the Practicalities chapter and RickSteves.com, which has helpful travel-tip articles and videos.

   Make sure your travel documents are valid. If your passport is due to expire within six months of your ticketed date of return, you need to renew it. Allow six weeks or more to renew or get a passport (www.travel.state.gov). Check for current Covid entry requirements, such as proof of vaccination or a negative Covid-19 test result.

   Arrange your transportation. Book your international flights. If you're traveling beyond Rome, research rail passes, train reservations, and car rentals.

Book rooms well in advance, especially if your trip falls during peak season or any major holidays or festivals.

Reserve ahead for key sights. Some sights require purchasing tickets online in advance: the Colosseum, Roman Forum, Palatine Hill, Vatican Museums, and Borghese Gallery. (The Vatican Museums don't technically require reservations, but they're essential to avoid time-consuming lines.) You must also reserve ahead online for the Pantheon on weekends. Clear instructions are in this guidebook. For all other sights, you can simply show up, pay, and enjoy.

Consider travel insurance. Compare the cost of insurance to the cost of your potential loss. Check whether your existing insurance (health, homeowners, or renters) covers you and your possessions overseas.

Call your bank. Alert your bank that you'll be using your debit and credit cards in Europe. Ask about transaction fees, and, if you don't already have one, get a "contactless" credit card (request your card PIN too). You don't need to bring euros along; you can withdraw euros from cash machines in Europe.

Use your smartphone smartly. Sign up for an international service plan to reduce your costs, or rely on Wi-Fi in Europe instead. Download any apps you'll want on the road, such as maps, translators, and Rick Steves Audio Europe (see sidebar on previous page).

Pack light. You'll walk with your luggage more than you think. I travel for weeks with a single carry-on bag and a day pack. Use the packing checklist later in this book as a guide.

Travel Smart

If you have a positive attitude, equip yourself with good information (this book), and expect to travel smart, you will.

Pickpockets abound in crowded places where tourists congregate. Treat commotions as smokescreens for theft. Keep your cash, credit cards, and passport secure in a money belt tucked under your clothes; carry only a day's spending money in your front pocket or wallet.

If you wilt easily, choose a hotel with air-conditioning, start your day early, take a midday siesta, and resume your sightseeing later.

Be sure to schedule in slack time for picnics, laundry, people-watching, leisurely dinners, shopping, and recharging your touristic batteries. Slow down and be open to unexpected experiences and the hospitality of the Roman people.

Sip an *aperitivo* on an atmospheric square, marvel at Rome's ancient structures, or grab a gelato and join the evening *passeggiata*. As you visit places I know and love, I'm happy you'll be meeting some of my favorite Romans.

Happy travels! *Buon viaggio!*

Heart of Rome Walk

From Campo de' Fiori to the Spanish Steps

Rome's most colorful neighborhood features narrow lanes, intimate piazzas, fanciful fountains, and some of Europe's best people-watching. During the day, this walk shows off the colorful Campo de' Fiori market and trendy boutiques as it meanders past major monuments such as the Pantheon and the Spanish Steps.

But the sunset brings unexpected magic. Sit so close to a bubbling fountain that traffic noise evaporates. Jostle with kids to see the gelato flavors. Watch lovers straddling more than the bench. And marvel at the ramshackle elegance that softens this brutal city. These are the flavors of Rome, best tasted after dark.

▶ *Start this mile-long walk at the Campo de' Fiori. The transportation hub Largo Argentina (buses #40, #64, and #492; tram #8; and taxis) is five blocks west. This walk is equally pleasant in reverse order—Start at Metro: Spanish Steps and finish at Campo de' Fiori, my favorite outdoor dining room after dark (for recommendations, see the Eating chapter). My free 🎧 Rick Steves audio tour covers this walk plus some additional stops.*

THE WALK BEGINS

❶ Campo de' Fiori

One of Rome's most colorful spots, this bohemian piazza hosts a fruit-and-vegetable market in the morning. In the evening, the cafés and restaurants that line the square predominate. On weekend nights, beer-drinking young people pack the medieval square, transforming it into a vast Roman street party.

This piazza has been the neighborhood's living room for centuries. In ancient times, it was a pleasant meadow—a *campo de' fiori*, or "field

Campo de' Fiori's raucous morning market, overseen by a statue of the rebel Giordano Bruno

of flowers." Then the Romans built a massive entertainment complex, the Theater of Pompey, right next to it, stretching from here to Largo Argentina (and including the spot where Julius Caesar was stabbed to death). In medieval times, Christian pilgrims passed through the *campo* on their way to the Vatican, and a thriving market developed.

Lording over the center of the square is the statue of **Giordano Bruno,** an intellectual who was burned here in 1600. The pedestal shows scenes from Bruno's trial and execution, and an inscription translates, "And the flames rose up." The statue, facing a Vatican administration building, was erected in 1889. Vatican officials protested the heretic in their midst, but they were overruled by angry neighborhood locals.

▶ *Exit the square in front of Bruno, turning right on Via dei Baullari. After about 200 yards, you'll cross busy Corso Vittorio Emanuele and enter a square with a statue of Marco Minghetti, an early Italian prime minister. Continue another 150 yards on Via di San Pantaleo, turn right at the beat-up old statue, and head up Via di Pasquino, emerging at...*

❷ Piazza Navona

This long, oblong square is dotted with fountains, busy with outdoor cafés, lined with palazzos and churches, and thronged with happy visitors. By its shape you might guess that it started out as a racetrack, built here around AD 80. But much of what we see today came in the 1600s, when the whole place got a major renovation.

Three Baroque fountains decorate the piazza. The most famous is in the center: the **Four Rivers Fountain** by Gian Lorenzo Bernini, the man who in the mid-1600s remade Rome in the Baroque style. Four burly river gods—representing the four quarters of the world—support an Egyptian-style obelisk. The good-looking figure of the Danube rep-

Piazza Navona—fountains and nightlife

Bernini's Four Rivers Fountain

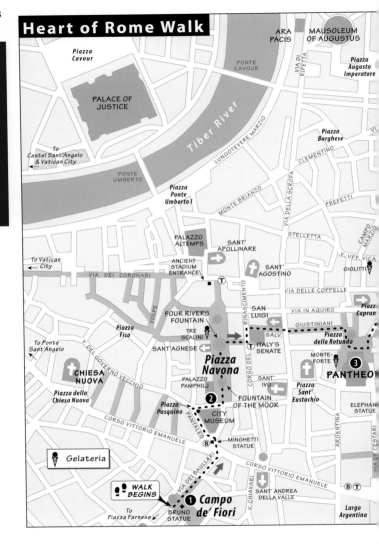

Heart of Rome Walk

ARA PACIS

MAUSOLEUM OF AUGUSTUS

Piazza Cavour

PONTE CAVOUR

VIA DI RIPETTA

Piazza Augusto Imperatore

PALACE OF JUSTICE

Tiber River

To Castel Sant'Angelo & Vatican City

LUNGOTEVERE MARZIO

Piazza Borghese

CLEMENTINO

PONTE UMBERTO

Piazza Ponte Umberto I

MONTE BRIANZO

VIA DELLA SCROFA

PREFETTI

STELLETTA

VI

PALAZZO ALTEMPS

SANT' APOLLINARE

CAMPO MARZIO

V. UFF. VICA

To Vatican City

VIA DEL CORONARI

ANCIENT STADIUM ENTRANCE

SANT' AGOSTINO

T

RINASCIMENTO

GIOLITTI

VIA DELLE COPPELLE

VOLPE

FOUR RIVERS FOUNTAIN

SAN LUIGI

VIA IN AQUIRO

Piazza Capran

Piazza Fico

TRE SCALINI

GIUSTINIANI

SALV.

Piazza della Rotunda

To Ponte Sant'Angelo

V. DEL GOVERNO VECCHIO

SANT'AGNESE

Piazza Navona

ITALY'S SENATE

T

CORSO DEL RINASCIMENTO

MONTE-FORTE

3

PANTHEO

CHIESA NUOVA

PALAZZO PAMPHILJ

SANT' IVO

Piazza Sant' Eustachio

Piazza della Chiesa Nuova

Piazza Pasquino

2

CITY MUSEUM

FOUNTAIN OF THE MOOR

ELEPHAN STATUE

CORSO VITTORIO EMANUELE

V. DEI BAULLARI

PANTALEO

B

MINGHETTI STATUE

ARGENTINA

VIA DE' CESTARI

Gelateria

CORSO VITTORIO EMANUELE

V. CHIAVARI

SANT'ANDREA DELLA VALLE

B T

WALK BEGINS

1 Campo de' Fiori

To Piazza Farnese

BRUNO STATUE

Largo Argentina

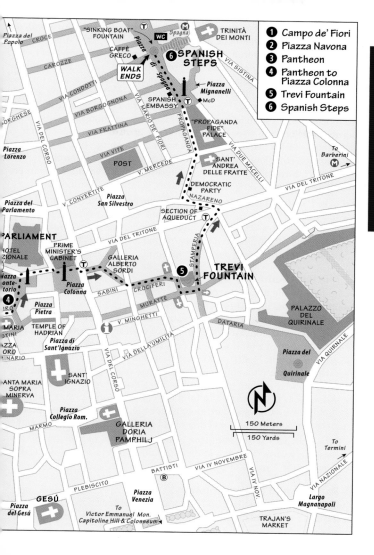

1 Campo de' Fiori
2 Piazza Navona
3 Pantheon
4 Pantheon to Piazza Colonna
5 Trevi Fountain
6 Spanish Steps

resents the continent of Europe. Next comes the Ganges (for Asia), a bearded old man with an oar between his legs. Next, the Nile (for Africa) has his head covered, since the river's source was unknown back then. Uruguay's Rio de la Plata, representing the Americas, tumbles backward in shock, wondering how he ever made the top four.

Now, follow the Plata river god's gaze upward. He's looking at the **Church of Sant'Agnese.** It was the work of Francesco Borromini, who was once Bernini's student and became his great rival. But legend says that Bernini designed the river god Plata to look up at Borromini's church... and tumble backward, in horror. It makes a great story... but, in fact, the fountain was completed before Borromini even began the church.

Piazza Navona is Rome's most interesting night scene, with street music, artists, fire-eaters, local Casanovas, gelato, and outdoor cafés.

▶ *Leave Piazza Navona directly across from Tre Scalini (famous for its chocolate gelato), and go east down Corsia Agonale, past rose peddlers and palm readers. Jog left around the guarded building (Palazzo Madama, where the Italian senate meets), and follow the brown Pantheon signs straight to Piazza della Rotunda and...*

❸ The Pantheon

Stand for a while under the portico, which is romantically floodlit and moonlit at night. The 40-foot, single-piece granite columns of the Pantheon's entrance show the scale the ancient Romans built on. The columns support a triangular Greek-style roof with an inscription that proclaims, "M. Agrippa built this." In fact, the present structure was built (*fecit*) by Emperor Hadrian (AD 120), who gave credit to the builder of an earlier temple. This impressive entranceway gives no clue that the greatest wonder of the building is inside—a domed room that inspired later domes. If it's open, pop in for a look around (on Sat-Sun you may need to book in advance). For more about the Pantheon's construction and interior, see page 138 or ∩ download my free Pantheon audio tour.

▶ *With your back to the Pantheon, veer to the right, heading uphill toward the yellow sign on Via degli Orfani that reads* Casa del Caffè *(marking the Tazza d'Oro coffee shop).*

❹ Pantheon to Piazza Colonna

Caffè Tazza d'Oro: This is one of Rome's top coffee shops, dating back to the days when this area was licensed to roast coffee beans. Locals

The Pantheon—the temple to "all the gods"—is now the focus of all the tourists.

come here for a shot of espresso or, when it's hot, a refreshing *granita di caffè con panna* (coffee and crushed ice with whipped cream).

▶ *Continue up Via degli Orfani to…*

Piazza Capranica: This square is home to the big, plain Florentine-Renaissance-style Palazzo Capranica (directly opposite as you enter the square). Its stubby tower was once much taller, but when a stronger government arrived, the nobles were all ordered to shorten their towers.

▶ *Leave the piazza to the right of the palazzo, heading down Via in Aquiro into a square called…*

Piazza di Montecitorio: This square, home to Italy's Parliament, is marked by an Egyptian obelisk from the sixth century BC. Emperor Augustus brought it to Rome as a trophy proclaiming his victory over Mark Antony and Cleopatra. Follow the zodiac markings in the pavement to the square's next big sight—the Italian Parliament. This impressive building is where the legislature's lower chamber (the equivalent of the US House of Representatives) attempts to govern the nation.

▶ *To your right is Piazza Colonna, where we're heading next—unless you like gelato (a one-block detour to the left brings you to a famous Roman gelateria, Giolitti).*

Piazza Colonna and Via del Corso: Piazza Colonna features a massive column that has stood here since the second century AD. The reliefs tell the story of Emperor Marcus Aurelius heroically battling barbarians around AD 170. The column is pure propaganda—in reality, the barbarians were winning, beginning Rome's long, three-century fall. The big white building adjacent to the parliament houses the prime minister's cabinet.

Beyond Piazza Colonna runs noisy Via del Corso, Rome's main north-south boulevard. For 2,000 years, all travelers from northern Europe first entered Rome on this street. The street was renamed "corso" for a famous medieval horse race that took place here during the crazy Carnevale season leading up to Lent. In 1854, Via del Corso became one of Rome's first gas-lit streets. It still hosts some of the city's most chic stores. Every evening, the pedestrian-only stretch of the Corso is packed with people on parade, taking to the streets for their *passeggiata* (see the "Dolce Vita Stroll" on page 147).

▶ *Cross Via del Corso to enter a big palatial building with columns, the Galleria Alberto Sordi shopping mall. Inside, take the fork to the right and exit out the back. (After 21:00, when the mall is closed, circle around the right side of the Galleria on Via dei Sabini.) The tourist kitsch builds as you head up Via de Crociferi to the roar of the water, lights, and people at the...*

❺ Trevi Fountain

The Trevi Fountain is the ultimate showcase for Rome's love affair with water. Architect Nicola Salvi conceived this liquid Baroque avalanche in 1762, cleverly incorporating the palace behind the fountain as a theatrical backdrop. Centerstage is the enormous figure known simply as the "Ocean." He symbolizes water in every form. The statue stands in his shell-shaped chariot, surfing through his wet dream. Water gushes from 24 spouts and tumbles over 30 different kinds of plants.

The square that faces the fountain has a lively atmosphere. The magic is enhanced by the fact that no streets directly approach it. You can hear the excitement as you draw near, and then—*bam!*—you're there. Enjoy the scene. Lucky Romeos clutch dates while unlucky suitors clutch beers.

Romantics toss a coin over their shoulder into the fountain. Legend says it will assure your return to Rome. Over the years, more convoluted legends sprang up—two coins bring romance, three means marriage...and

The Trevi Fountain—make a wish, toss a coin, and dream.

no coins means you're divorced and paying alimony. It's all pretty silly. But hey—it's Rome, and the world is yours. Make up your own wish.

▶ *From the Trevi Fountain, it's 10 minutes to our next stop, the Spanish Steps. Facing the Trevi Fountain, go forward, walking along the right side of the fountain on Via della Stamperia. Cross the busy Via del Tritone. Continue 100 yards and veer right at Via delle Fratte, a street that changes its name to Via Propaganda before opening up into Piazza di Spagna and the climax of our walk.*

❻ Spanish Steps

The wide, curving staircase is one of Rome's iconic sights. Its 138 steps lead sharply up from Piazza di Spagna. The design culminates at the top in an obelisk framed between two Baroque church towers. The square and its famous steps are called "Spanish" thanks to the Spanish embassy to the Vatican across the way.

For decades the steps were a favorite Roman hangout, but recently the city banned anyone from sitting on them. You can walk up and down the steps, but if you sit, you'll face a €250 fine.

At the foot of the steps is the aptly named Sinking Boat Fountain. It was built by Gian Lorenzo Bernini's father, Pietro. Because the water

The Spanish Steps—less a historic monument than a fine place for a walk

pressure here is low, the water can't shoot high in the air. So Bernini designed the fountain to be low key—a sinking boat filled with water.

The Piazza di Spagna has been the hangout of many Romantics over the years (Keats, Wagner, Openshaw, Goethe, and others). British poet John Keats pondered his mortality, then died of tuberculosis at age 25 in the orange building on the right side of the steps. Fellow Romantic Lord Byron lived across the square at #66.

The piazza is a thriving scene both day and night. Before you head off, take a final 360-degree spin. This space features many of the themes we've enjoyed on this walk—fountains, obelisks, public spaces, statues, and gelato. Most of all, it's a glimpse at today's Rome—a city where friends and families live much the same kind of life as their ancient cousins.

▶ *Our walk is finished. To reach the top of the steps sweat-free, take the free elevator just inside the Spagna Metro stop (to the left, as you face the steps; elevator closes at 23:30). When you're ready to leave, you can zip home on the Metro or grab a taxi at the north or south ends of the piazza.*

Colosseum Tour

Colosseo

Start your visit to Rome with its iconic symbol—the Colosseum. Fifty thousand Romans could pack this huge stadium and cheer as their favorite gladiators faced off in bloody battles to the death.

This self-guided tour brings that ancient world to life—the world of Caesars, slaves, Vestal Virgins, trumpet fanfares, roaring lions, and hordes of rabid fans. Prowl the arena like gladiators, climb to the cheap seats for the view, see the underground "backstage" where they kept caged animals, and marvel at the engineering prowess that allowed these ancient people to build on such a colossal scale.

For its thrilling history and sheer massiveness, the Colosseum gets a unanimous thumbs-up.

ORIENTATION

Cost: €18 **basic ticket** covers the Colosseum and the Roman Forum/
Palatine Hill (valid 24 hours); the €24 **Full Experience ticket** covers all three sights and adds access to the Colosseum's arena floor
(valid 48 hours; also includes a few lesser sights at the Forum and
Palatine Hill).

Mandatory Advance Ticketing: Tickets must be purchased in advance to get a reserved Colosseum entry time (Coopculture.it, select English, and click on Ticketing; you'll be emailed a ticket/QR
code to use at entry). You can also book by phone (see below under
"Information").

Hours: Daily from 9:00 until one hour before sunset: April-Aug until
19:15, Sept until 19:00, Oct until 18:30, Nov-Feb until 16:30, March
until 17:30; last entry one hour before closing.

Information: +39 06 3996 7700 (English spoken, daily 10:00-15:00),
www.parcocolosseo.it.

When to Go: Try to get an early-morning or late-afternoon time slot.
At midday, the Colosseum can be so crowded that even reservation
holders can face long waits. If you show up without a reservation
you could join one of the tours sold by hawkers outside the gate as
a last resort. Generally, crowds are thinner in the afternoon.

Getting There: Metro Colosseo or buses #51, #75, #85, #87, and #118.

Tours: ∩ Download my free Colosseum audio tour. For more, a fact-
filled audioguide (€5.50/1 hour) and a handheld videoguide (€6/50
minutes) are available just past the turnstiles. Official guided tours
in English depart regularly (€10, smart to book in advance with
your admission—they sell out). Private guides stand outside the
Colosseum looking for business (€25-30/2-hour tour of the Colosseum, Forum, and Palatine Hill).

Length of This Tour: Allow an hour.

Restoration: A multiyear renovation project may affect your visit.

Nearby: It makes sense to see the Colosseum together with the Roman
Forum and Palatine Hill, which are just next door and covered by
a joint ticket.

THE TOUR BEGINS

▶ *There it is! View the Colosseum from the Forum fence, across the street from the Colosseo Metro station.*

Exterior

Built when the Roman Empire was at its peak in AD 80, the Colosseum represents Rome at its grandest. The Flavian Amphitheater (the Colosseum's real name) was an arena for gladiator contests and public spectacles. When killing became a spectator sport, the Romans wanted to share the fun with as many people as possible, so they stuck two semicircular theaters together to create a freestanding amphitheater, the largest in the empire.

The sheer size of the Colosseum is impressive, even in our era of mega-stadiums. With four oversized stories, it's 160 feet high, nearly a third of a mile around, and makes an oval-shaped footprint that covers six acres.

The stadium could accommodate 50,000 roaring fans (that's 100,000 thumbs). As Romans arrived for the games, they'd be greeted outside by a huge bronze statue of the emperor Nero—100 feet tall, gleaming in the sunlight.

The Colosseum's facade says a lot about the Roman personality. The Romans were engineers more than artists, so they borrowed decorative elements from the more cultured Greeks. Look closely at the half-columns that flank the arches. These ornamental columns have no structural purpose, and are done in the Greek style: sturdy Doric on the ground level, scroll-shaped Ionic on the second story, leafy Corinthian on the next level. By combining these classy Greek elements with pragmatic Roman engineering, the builders added a veneer of sophistication

Eternal crowds in the Eternal City

A good guide adds context to your visit.

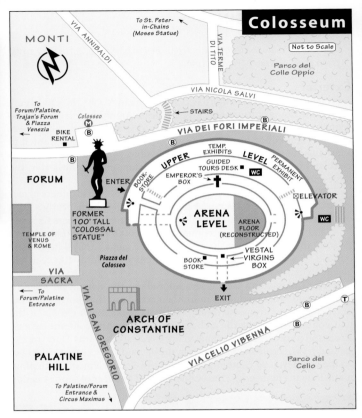

Not to Scale

MONTI

VIA ANNIBALDI

To St. Peter-
in-Chains
(Moses Statue)

VIA TERME
DI TITO

Parco del
Colle Oppio

VIA NICOLA SALVI

STAIRS

Colosseo
M

To
Forum/Palatine,
Trajan's Forum
& Piazza
Venezia

BIKE
RENTAL

VIA DEI FORI IMPERIALI

FORUM

ENTER

BOOK-STORE

UPPER   LEVEL

TEMP.
EXHIBITS

GUIDED
TOURS DESK

EMPEROR'S
BOX

PERMANENT
EXHIBIT

WC

ELEVATOR

FORMER
100' TALL
"COLOSSAL
STATUE"

ARENA
LEVEL

ARENA
FLOOR
(RECONSTRUCTED)

WC

TEMPLE OF
VENUS
& ROME

Piazza del
Colosseo

BOOK-
STORE

VESTAL
VIRGINS
BOX

VIA
SACRA

To
Forum/Palatine
Entrance

VIA DI SAN GREGORIO

EXIT

ARCH OF
CONSTANTINE

B

T

PALATINE
HILL

VIA CELIO VIBENNA

Parco del
Celio

To Palatine/Forum
Entrance &
Circus Maximus

to this arena of death.

Of the 250 or so amphitheaters in the Roman Empire, this was the granddaddy of them all—the biggest, the most famous, and with all the top-notch gladiators. Today, only a third of the original Colosseum remains. Earthquakes destroyed some of it, but most was carted off during the Middle Ages and Renaissance as easy precut stone for other buildings.

▶ *To enter, line up, show your ticket/QR code, and pass through security.*

Ground Level

Once past the turnstiles, signs direct you to the official visitors' route; depending on current policies, you may be able to explore in whatever order you like. Even if you aren't required to, following the official route ensures you will see everything. (If following signs, you want the "long route," which includes the upstairs—with the best views.)

▶ *Wherever you spill out into the arena, just take it all in and get oriented. The tallest side of the Colosseum (with the large Christian cross) is the north side.*

Entering the Stadium

Imagine being an ancient spectator arriving for the games. Fans could pour in through ground-floor entrances; there were 76 numbered ones in addition to the emperor's private entrance on the north side. Your ticket (likely a pottery shard) was marked with your entrance, section, row, and seat number. You'd pass by concession stands selling fast food and souvenirs, such as wine glasses with the names of famous gladiators. A hallway leading to the seats was called a *vomitorium*. At exit time, the Colosseum would "vomit" out its contents, giving us the English word. It's estimated that a capacity crowd could enter and exit in just 15 minutes.

Arena

The games took place in this oval-shaped arena, 280 feet long by 165 feet wide. The ratio of length to width is close to the so-called golden ratio. Since the days of the Greek mathematician Pythagoras, artists considered that proportion (1.6 to 1) to be ideal.

When you look down into the arena, you're seeing the underground passages beneath the playing surface (which can be visited only on a private tour). The arena was originally covered with a wooden floor, then sprinkled with sand (*arena* in Latin). The bit of reconstructed floor gives you an accurate sense of the original arena level and the subterranean warren where animals and prisoners were held. As in modern stadiums, the spectators ringed the playing area in bleacher seats that slanted up from the arena floor. Around you are the big brick masses that supported the tiers of seats.

A variety of materials were used to build the stadium. Look around. Big white travertine blocks stacked on top of each other formed the skeleton. The pillars for the bleachers were made with a shell of brick,

Modern Amenities in the Ancient World

The area around the Colosseum, Forum, and Palatine Hill is rich in history but pretty barren when it comes to food, shelter, and WCs. Here are a few options:

The Colosseum has a crowded **WC** inside and a pay WC outside the arena's east end. If you can wait, Palatine Hill has several good WCs—at the Via di San Gregorio entrance, in the museum, near the stadium, near the entry to the Forum, and in the Farnese Gardens. The Forum has WCs at the entrance on Via dei Fori Imperiali and in the middle of the Forum (near #3 on the map on page 31).

Because **eating** options are limited, consider bringing a snack. The Colosseo Metro stop has forgettable hot sandwiches and sells drinks. A few of my recommended restaurants are within a few blocks (see page 187). The Monti neighborhood, with several recommended eateries, is just north of the Forum's Via dei Fori Imperiali entrance.

To refill your **water** bottle, stop at a fountain next to the Colosseo Metro entrance, or inside the Colosseum, Forum, and Palatine Hill.

A nice oasis is the free **information center** located across from the Forum entrance on Via dei Fori Imperiali and a bit east, toward the Colosseum (small café, food stand, WC; open daily 9:30-19:00). If you're on **Capitoline Hill,** you'll find services at the Capitoline Museums, including a nice view café (see page 131).

Public buses (#85, #87, etc.) traverse Via dei Fori Imperiali between the Colosseum and Piazza Venezia, making it easy to hop on for a stop or two. For a **taxi,** use the stand near the Colosseum's southeast corner. (Taxis parked near the Colosseo Metro stop on Via dei Fori Imperiali have a bad reputation.)

filled in with concrete. Originally the bare brick was covered with marble columns or ornamental facing, so the interior was a brilliant white (they used white plaster for the upper-floor cheap seats).

The Colosseum's seating was strictly segregated. At ringside, the emperor, senators, Vestal Virgins, and VIPs occupied marble seats with their names carved on them (a few marble seats have been restored, at the east end). The next level up held those of noble birth. The level tourists now occupy was for ordinary free Roman citizens, called plebeians. Up at the very top (a hundred yards from the action), there were

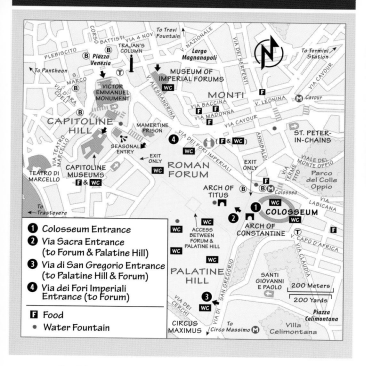

1 Colosseum Entrance
2 Via Sacra Entrance
(to Forum & Palatine Hill)
3 Via di San Gregorio Entrance
(to Palatine Hill & Forum)
4 Via dei Fori Imperiali
Entrance (to Forum)

F Food
● Water Fountain

once wooden bleachers for the poorest people—foreigners, slaves, and women. While no seats survive, you can imagine the scene.

Picture the awning that could be stretched across the top of the stadium by armies of sailors. The awning covered only about a third of the arena—so those at the top always enjoyed shade, while many nobles down below roasted in the sun.

Looking into the complex web of passageways beneath the arena, imagine how busy the backstage action was. Gladiators strolled down the central corridor, from their warm-up yard on the east end to the

The arena had underground passageways, where gladiators warmed up amid caged animals.

arena entrance on the west. Some workers tended wild animals. Others prepared stage sets of trees or fake buildings, allowing the arena to be quickly transformed from an African jungle to a Greek temple. Props and sets were hauled up to arena level on 80 different elevator shafts via a system of ropes and pulleys. (You might be able to make out some small rectangular shafts, especially near the center of the arena.) That means there were 80 different spots from which animals, warriors, and stage sets could pop up and magically appear.

The Games

The games began with a few warm-up acts—dogs attacking porcupines, female gladiators battling each other, or a one-legged man fighting a dwarf. Then came the main event: the gladiators. Trumpets would blare, drums would pound, and the gladiators would enter the arena from the west end, parade around to the music, and pause at the south side. There, they'd acknowledge the Vestal Virgins sitting in their special box seats on the 50-yard line. After a nod to the Virgins, the gladiators continued on to the emperor's box. There, they'd raise their weap-

Column capital of marble

The top story once held an awning.

ons, salute, and shout *Ave, Caesar!*—"Hail Caesar! We who are about to die salute you!" (Though some scholars doubt they actually said that.)

These warriors had their own martial specialties. Some carried swords, protected only with a shield and a heavy helmet. Some threw the javelin. Others represented fighting fishermen, with a net to snare opponents and a trident to spear them. The gladiators were usually slaves, criminals, or poor people who saw a chance for freedom, wealth, and fame in the ring. They learned to fight in training schools, then battled their way up the ranks. The best were rewarded very much like our modern sports stars, with fan clubs, great wealth, and, yes, product endorsements.

If a gladiator fell helpless to the ground, his opponent would approach the emperor's box and ask: Should he live or should he die? Sometimes the emperor or master of ceremonies would leave the decision to the crowd, who would judge how valiantly the man had fought and delivered the verdict—thumbs-up or thumbs-down. (Scholars debate exactly which gesture meant what.) The Romans thought nothing of condemning a coward to the death he deserved.

Consider the value of these games in placating and controlling the huge Roman populace. In an age without a hint of a newsreel, it was hard for local Romans to visualize and appreciate the faraway conquests of their empire. The Colosseum spectacles were a way to bring home the environments, animals, and people of these conquered lands; parade them before the public; and make them real. Imagine never having seen an actual lion, and suddenly one jumps out to chase a prisoner in the arena. Seeing the king of beasts slain by a gladiator reminded the masses of man's triumph over nature.

A cross marks the emperor's box.

Arch of Constantine—Christianity triumphs

And having the thumbs-up or thumbs-down authority over another person's life gave the spectators a real sense of power. Think of the psychological boost the otherwise downtrodden masses felt when the emperor granted them this thrilling decision.

Did the Romans throw Christians to the lions as in the movies? Christians were definitely thrown to the lions, made to fight gladiators, crucified, and burned alive...but probably not here in this particular stadium. Maybe, but probably not.

Rome was a nation of warriors that built an empire by conquest. The battles fought against barbarians, Egyptians, and strange animals were played out daily here in the Colosseum for the benefit of city-slicker bureaucrats, who got vicarious thrills by watching brutes battle to the death. The contests were always free, sponsored by the government to bribe the people's favor or to keep Rome's growing masses of unemployed rabble off the streets.

▶ *If you paid for the* **Full Experience ticket,** *continue past these stairs to go out into the arena for an awe-inspiring view of the Colosseum from the gladiator's perspective (then circle back to the stairs). If you purchased the* **basic ticket,** *no problem—the views from up top, available to everyone, are plenty thrilling. Climb the stairs and tour the...*

Upper Level

Permanent Exhibit

The permanent exhibit, with lots of ancient artifacts found on-site, architectural illustrations, and fascinating reconstruction models (all well described in English), helps bring the place to life. You'll learn about pulleys and hoists, ancient pastimes, and Roman seating hierarchy. The huge, cutaway model of the intact Colosseum is worth lingering over.

▶ *As you roam about, be sure to find a spot at the west end of the upper deck, where you can look out over some of the sights nearby. Start your visual tour of sights that ring the Colosseum with the big, white, triumphal arch.*

Arch of Constantine

This arch marks one of the great turning points in history—the military coup that made Christianity mainstream. In AD 312, Emperor Constantine defeated his rival Maxentius in the crucial Battle of the Milvian Bridge. The night before, he had seen a vision of a cross in the sky. Constantine—whose mother and sister had already become Christians—became sole emperor and legalized Christianity. With this one battle, a once-obscure Jewish sect with a handful of followers became the state religion of the entire Western world. In AD 300, you could be killed for being a Christian; a century later, you could be killed for not being one. Church enrollment boomed.

Surrounding Hills

The Colosseum stands in a valley between three of Rome's legendary seven hills. Palatine Hill rises to the southwest, beyond the Arch of Constantine, dotted with umbrella pines. The Caelian is to the south and the Esquiline is to the north. Next to the Arch of Constantine is the road called the Via Sacra, or Sacred Way, once Rome's main street, that leads uphill from the Colosseum to the Forum.

▶ *Looking west, in the direction of the Forum, you'll see some ruins sitting atop a raised, rectangular-shaped hill. The ruins—consisting of an arched alcove made of brick and backed by a church bell tower—are all that remain of the once-great...*

Temple of Venus and Rome

At 100 feet tall, this temple atop a pedestal was one of the most prominent temples in Rome—and also its biggest. The size of a football field, it once covered the entire hill.

The main ruin in the center—the tall brick arch with a cross-hatched ceiling—was once the *cella,* or sacred chamber of the temple. Here sat two monumental statues, back to back. Venus, the goddess of

Temple of Venus and Rome

love, faced the Colosseum. The goddess called Roma Aeterna faced the Forum. The pair of statues symbolized the birth and eternal destiny of the race of people meant to endure forever.

In ancient times, newlyweds ascended the staircase from the Colosseum (some parts are still visible) to the temple to ask Venus and Roma Aeterna to bring them good luck. These days, Roman couples get married at the adjacent church with the bell tower to ensure themselves love and happiness for eternity.

The Colosseum's Legacy

With the coming of Christianity to Rome, the Colosseum and its deadly games slowly became recognized as barbaric. As the Roman Empire dwindled and the infrastructure crumbled, the stadium itself was neglected. Finally, around AD 523—after nearly 500 years of games—the Colosseum shut its doors.

Over time, the Colosseum was eroded by wind, rain, and the strain of gravity. Earthquakes weakened it, and a powerful quake in 1349 toppled the south side.

More than anything, the Colosseum was dismantled by Rome's citizens themselves, who carted off precut stones for the construction of palaces and churches, including St. Peter's. The marble facing was

A Page of History

Ancient Rome (500 BC–AD 500): Legend says that Romulus and Remus—twins orphaned at birth and raised by a she-wolf—founded Rome in 753 BC. From humble beginnings, the city expanded, through conquest and trade, to dominate the Italian peninsula and beyond.

By AD 100, Rome was master of Western Europe and the Mediterranean. Booty and captured slaves poured in. The former Republic (governed by a senate) was now an empire of 54 million people. The city of Rome, population 1.2 million, was dotted with monumental sports stadiums, baths, aqueducts, and temples—the wonder of the age.

Corruption, disease, and barbarian attacks slowly drained the unwieldy empire. Though Emperor Constantine brought temporary stability and legalized Christianity (in 313 AD), Rome eventually fell to invaders (AD 476), plunging Europe into chaos.

Medieval (AD 500–1500): The once-great city dwindled to a rough village of overgrown ruins. During the 1300s, even the popes left Rome to live in France. What little glory Rome retained was in the pomp, knowledge, and wealth of the Catholic Church.

Renaissance (1500s): As Europe's economy recovered, energetic popes rebuilt Rome, including the new St. Peter's Basilica.

Baroque and Neoclassical (1600–1900): The city was no longer a great political force, but it remained the influential capital of Catholicism during the struggle against Protestants. To attract pilgrims, popes further beautified the city, in the Baroque and Neoclassical styles: St. Peter's Square, ornate church interiors, Bernini's statues, and the Trevi Fountain. In 1871, modern Italy was formed under King Victor Emmanuel II, and—naturally—Rome was named its capital.

War, Fascism, Revival (1900s): Italy's fascist dictator Benito Mussolini modernized Rome with broad boulevards and the Metro system. He also dragged Italy into WWII's destruction, though the city's monuments were spared. Postwar Italy suffered through government-a-year chaos and Mafia-tainted corruption. But its "economic miracle" made Rome a world-class city of cinema (Fellini), banking, and tourism.

Rome Today: Today, the city's monuments are spruced up, even if its economy—and soccer teams—sometimes sputter. Rome is ready for pilgrims, travelers…and you.

pulverized into mortar, and 300 tons of iron brackets were pried out and melted down, resulting in the pockmarking you see today.

After centuries of neglect, a series of 16th-century popes took pity on the pagan structure. In memory of the Christians who may (or may not) have been martyred here, they shored up the south and west sides with bricks and placed the big cross on the north side of the arena.

Today, the Colosseum links Rome's glorious past with its vital present. Major political demonstrations begin or end here, providing protesters with an iconic backdrop for the TV cameras. On Good Friday, the pope comes here to lead pilgrims as they follow the Stations of the Cross.

The legend goes that as long as the Colosseum shall stand, the city of Rome shall also stand. For nearly 2,000 years, the Colosseum has been the enduring symbol of Rome, the Eternal City.

Roman Forum Tour

Foro Romano

For nearly a thousand years, the Forum was the vital heart of Rome. Nestled in Rome's famous seven hills, this is the Eternal City's birthplace. While only broken columns and arches remain of the Forum today, this tour helps resurrect the rubble.

Stroll down main street, where shoppers in togas once came to browse and gawk at towering temples and triumphal arches. See where senators passed laws and where orators mounted a rostrum to address their friends, Romans, and countrymen. Visit the temple where Vestal Virgins tended a sacred flame and the spot where Julius Caesar's body was burned. In the middle of it all, you'll still find the main square where ancient citizens once passed the time, just as Romans do in piazzas today.

Cost: €18 for basic ticket, which also includes the Colosseum and Palatine Hill (valid 24 hours); €24 Full Experience ticket covers all three sights (valid 48 hours; includes a few lesser sights as well).

Mandatory Advance Ticketing: Tickets must be booked in advance at Coopculture.it (no on-site sales). For ticketing details, see page 26.

Hours: Daily from 9:00 until one hour before sunset: April-Aug until 19:15, Sept until 19:00, Oct until 18:30, Nov-Feb until 16:30, March until 17:30; last entry one hour before closing.

Information: +39 06 3996 7700 (English spoken, daily 10:00-15:00), www.parcocolosseo.it.

Getting In: There are three main entrances to the Forum/Palatine Hill sight: 1) from the Colosseum—nearest the Arch of Titus; 2) from Via dei Fori Imperiali; and 3) from Via di San Gregorio—at south end of Palatine Hill. At busy times, turnstiles farther up Via dei Fori Imperiali, near the Arch of Septimius Severus, are sometimes open.

Tours: ∩ Download my free Roman Forum **audio tour,** which offers a concise introduction to the sight. Audioguides or a downloadable app may be available to further decipher the rubble.

Length of This Tour: Allow 1.5 hours.

Services: For food and WCs in the area, see page 30.

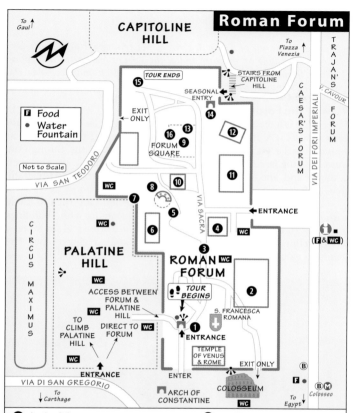

1. Arch of Titus
2. Basilica of Constantine
3. Via Sacra
4. Temple of Antoninus Pius & Faustina
5. Temple of Vesta
6. House of the Vestal Virgins
7. Caligula's Palace
8. Temple of Castor & Pollux
9. The Forum's Main Square
10. Temple of Julius Caesar
11. Basilica Aemilia
12. The Curia
13. Rostrum
14. Arch of Septimius Severus
15. Temple of Saturn
16. Column of Phocas

THE TOUR BEGINS

▶ *Start at the Arch of Titus. It's the white triumphal arch that rises above the rubble on the east end of the Forum (closest to the Colosseum). Stand at the viewpoint alongside the arch and gaze over the valley known as the Roman Forum.*

View of the Forum

The Forum is a rectangular valley running roughly east (the Colosseum end) to west (Capitoline Hill, with its bell tower). The rocky path at your feet is the Via Sacra. It leads from the Arch of Titus, through the trees, past the large brick Senate building, through the triumphal arch at the far end, and up Capitoline Hill. The hill to your left (with all the trees) is Palatine Hill.

Picture being here when a conquering general returned to Rome with crates of booty. The valley was full of gleaming white buildings topped with bronze roofs. The Via Sacra—the Forum's Main Street— would be lined with citizens waving branches and carrying torches. The trumpets would sound as the parade began.

The overgrown rubble of the Forum is nestled in a valley at the base of Capitoline Hill.

Rome: Republic and Empire (500 BC-AD 500)

Ancient Rome lasted for a thousand years, from about 500 BC to AD 500. During that time, Rome expanded from a small tribe of barbarians to a vast empire, then dwindled slowly to city size again. For the first 500 years, when Rome's armies made her ruler of the Italian peninsula and beyond, Rome was a republic governed by elected senators. Over the next 500 years, a time of world conquest and eventual decline, Rome was an empire ruled by a military-backed dictator.

Julius Caesar bridged the gap between republic and empire. This ambitious general and politician, popular with the people because of his military victories and charisma, suspended the Roman constitution and assumed dictatorial powers in about 50 BC. A few years later, he was assassinated by a conspiracy of senators. His adopted son, Augustus, succeeded him, and soon "Caesar" was not just a name but a title.

Emperor Augustus ushered in the Pax Romana, or Roman peace (AD 1-200), a time when Rome reached her peak and controlled an empire that stretched even beyond Eurail—from England to Egypt, Turkey to Morocco.

First came porters, carrying chests full of gold and jewels. Then, a parade of exotic animals from the conquered lands—elephants, giraffes, hippopotamuses—for the crowd to "ooh" and "ahh" at. Next came the prisoners in chains, with the captive king on a wheeled platform so the people could jeer and spit at him. Finally, the conquering hero himself would drive down in his four-horse chariot, with rose petals strewn in his path. The whole procession would run the length of the Forum and up the face of Capitoline Hill to the Temple of Saturn (the eight big columns midway up the hill—#15 on the map), where they'd place the booty in Rome's coffers.

Then they'd continue up to the summit to the Temple of Jupiter (only ruins of its foundation remain—within the Capitoline Museums) to dedicate the victory to the king of the gods.

❶ Arch of Titus (Arco di Tito)

The Arch of Titus commemorated the Roman victory over the province of Judaea (Israel) in AD 70. The Romans had a reputation as benevolent conquerors who tolerated local customs and rulers. All they required

After Titus conquered the Jews, he made them build his victory monument—the Arch of Titus.

was allegiance to the empire, shown by worshipping the emperor as a god. No problem for most conquered people, who already had half a dozen gods on their prayer lists anyway. But Israelites believed in only one god, and it wasn't the emperor. Israel revolted. After a short but bitter war, the Romans defeated the rebels, took Jerusalem, destroyed their temple (leaving only a fragment of one wall's foundation—today's revered "Wailing Wall"), and brought home 50,000 Jewish slaves...who were forced to build this arch (and the Colosseum).

Roman propaganda decorates the inside of the arch, where a relief shows the emperor Titus in a chariot being crowned by the goddess Victory. The other side shows booty from the sacking of the temple in Jerusalem—soldiers carrying a Jewish menorah and other plunder. The two (unfinished) plaques on poles were to have listed the conquered cities. Look at the top of the ceiling. Constructed after Titus' death, the relief shows him riding an eagle to heaven, where he'll become one of the gods.

The brutal crushing of the AD 70 rebellion (and another one 60 years later) devastated the nation of Israel. There would be no Jewish political entity again for almost 2,000 years, until modern Israel was created after World War II.

▶ *Walk down Via Sacra into the Forum. After about 50 yards, turn right and follow a path uphill to the three huge arches of the...*

❷ Basilica of Constantine (Basilica Maxentius)

Yes, these are big arches. But they represent only one-third of the original Basilica of Constantine, a mammoth hall of justice. The arches were matched by a similar set along the Via Sacra side (only a few squat brick piers remain). Between them ran the central hall, which was spanned by a roof 130 feet high—about 55 feet higher than the side arches you see.

The hall itself was as long as a football field, lavishly furnished (with colorful inlaid marble, a gilded bronze ceiling, and statues), and filled with strolling Romans. At the far (west) end was an enormous marble statue of Emperor Constantine on a throne. (Pieces of this statue, including a hand the size of a man, are on display in Rome's Capitoline Museums.)

▶ *Now backtrack downhill and stroll deeper into the Forum, turning right along the...*

❸ Via Sacra

Stroll through the trees, down this main drag of the ancient city. Imagine being an out-of-town visitor during Rome's heyday. You know a little Latin, but nothing would have prepared you for the bustle of Rome—a city of a million people, by far the biggest in Europe. This street would be swarming with tribunes, slaves, and courtesans. Chariots whizzed by. Wooden stalls lined the roads, where merchants peddled their goods.

On your right, you'll pass a building with a green door still swinging on its fourth-century hinges—the original bronze door to a temple that survived because it became a church shortly after the fall of Rome.

These arches are all that remain...

...of the once-grand Basilica of Constantine.

▶ *Just past the ancient temple, 10 huge columns stand in front of a much newer-looking church. This colonnade was part of the...*

❹ Temple of Antoninus Pius and Faustina

The Senate built this temple to honor Emperor Antoninus Pius (AD 138-161) and his deified wife, Faustina. The 50-foot-tall Corinthian (leafy) columns must have been awe-inspiring to out-of-towners who grew up in thatched huts. Although the temple has been inhabited by a church, you can still see the basic layout—a staircase led to a shaded porch (the columns), which admitted you to the main building (now a church), where the statue of the god sat.

Picture these columns with gilded capitals supporting brightly painted statues in a triangular pediment, and the whole building capped with a gleaming bronze roof. The stately gray rubble of today's Forum is a faded black-and-white photograph of a 3-D Technicolor era.

▶ *With your back to the colonnade, walk straight ahead—jogging a bit to the right to stay on the path. The path leads to two sights associated with Rome's Vestal Virgins. Head for the three short columns connected by a wall, all that's left of the...*

❺ Temple of Vesta

This is perhaps Rome's most sacred spot. Rome considered itself one big family, and inside this temple a fire burned, just as in a Roman home. Back in those days, you never wanted your fire to go out. As long as the sacred flame burned, Rome would stand. The flame was tended by six priestesses known as the Vestal Virgins.

▶ *Backtrack a few steps up the path, behind the Temple of Vesta. You'll find a few stairs that lead up to a big, enclosed field with two rectangular brick pools (just below the hill). This was the courtyard of the...*

❻ House of the Vestal Virgins

The Vestal Virgins lived in a two-story building surrounding a long central courtyard with two pools at one end. Rows of statues depicting leading Vestal Virgins flanked the courtyard. This place was the model—both architecturally and sexually—for medieval convents and monasteries.

Chosen from noble families before they reached the age of 10, the six Vestal Virgins each served a 30-year term. Honored and revered by the Romans, the Vestals even had their own box seats opposite the emperor in the Colosseum.

The Temple of Antoninus Pius and Faustina gives a glimpse of the Forum's former grandeur.

As the name implies, a Vestal took a vow of chastity. If she served her term faithfully—abstaining for 30 years—she was given a huge dowry and allowed to marry. But if they found any Virgin who wasn't, she was strapped to a funeral car, paraded through the streets of the Forum, taken to a crypt, given a loaf of bread and a lamp...and buried alive. Many Vestals suffered the latter fate.

▶ *Looming just beyond this field is Palatine Hill—the corner of which may have been...*

❼ Caligula's Palace (Palace of Tiberius)

Emperor Caligula (ruled AD 37-41) had a huge palace on Palatine Hill overlooking the Forum. It actually sprawled down the hill into the Forum (some supporting arches remain in the hillside).

Caligula was not a nice person. He tortured enemies, stole senators' wives, and parked his chariot in handicap spaces. But Rome's luxury-loving emperors only added to the glory of the Forum, with each one trying to make his mark on history.

▶ *Return to the three short columns of the Temple of Vesta. Just downhill, you can't miss three very tall columns just beyond.*

Temple of Vesta, tended by Vestal Virgins

Temple of Castor and Pollux

❽ Temple of Castor and Pollux

These three columns—all that remain of a once-prestigious temple—
have become the most photographed sight in the Forum. The temple
was one of the city's oldest, built in the fifth century BC. It commemorated the Roman victory over the Tarquin, the notorious Etruscan king
who once oppressed them. As a symbol of Rome's self-governing republic, the temple was often used as a meeting place of senators, and its
front steps served as a podium for free speech. The three columns are
Corinthian style, featuring leafy capitals and fluting. They date from a
later incarnation of the temple (first century).

▶ *Just beyond, the path spills into a flat, open area that stretches before
you. This was the center of the ancient Forum.*

❾ The Forum's Main Square

The original Forum, or main square, was this flat patch about the size of
a football field, stretching to the foot of Capitoline Hill. Surrounding it
were temples, law courts, government buildings, and triumphal arches.

Rome was born right here. According to legend, twin brothers
Romulus (Rome) and Remus were orphaned in infancy and raised by
a she-wolf on top of Palatine Hill. Growing up, they found it hard to
get dates. So, they and their cohorts attacked the nearby Sabine tribe
and kidnapped their women. After they made peace, this marshy
valley became the trading center for the scattered tribes on the surrounding hillsides.

The square was the busiest and most crowded—and often the
seediest—section of town. Besides senators, politicians, and currency
exchangers, there were even sleazier types—souvenir hawkers, pick-

Today's field of rubble...

...was once a gleaming canyon of marble.

pockets, fortune-tellers, gamblers, slave marketers, drunks, hookers, lawyers, and tour guides.

The Forum is now rubble, but imagine it in its prime: blindingly brilliant marble buildings with 40-foot-high columns and shining metal roofs; rows of statues painted in realistic colors; processional chariots rattling down Via Sacra. Mentally replace tourists in T-shirts with tribunes in togas. Imagine the buildings towering and the people buzzing around you while an orator gives a rabble-rousing speech from the Rostrum. If things still look like just a pile of rocks, at least tell yourself, "But Julius Caesar once leaned against these rocks."

▶ *And speaking of Julius Caesar, at the near end of the main square (the end closest to the Colosseum) find the foundations of a temple now sheltered by a peaked wood-and-metal roof.*

⑩ Temple of Julius Caesar (Tempio del Divo Giulio, or Ara di Cesare)

On March 15, in 44 BC, Julius Caesar was stabbed 23 times by political conspirators. After his assassination, Caesar's body was cremated on this spot (under the metal roof). Afterward, this temple was built to honor him.

Caesar (100-44 BC) changed Rome—and the Forum—dramatically. He cleared out many of the wooden market stalls and began to ring the square with even grander buildings. Caesar's house was located behind the temple, near that clump of trees. He walked right by here on the day he was assassinated ("Beware the Ides of March!" warned a street-corner Etruscan preacher).

Although he was popular with the masses, not everyone liked Caesar's urban design or his politics. When he assumed dictatorial powers, he was ambushed and stabbed to death by a conspiracy of senators, including his adopted son, Brutus (*"Et tu, Brute?"*).

The funeral was held here, facing the main square. The citizens gathered, and speeches were made. Mark Antony stood up to say (in Shakespeare's words), "Friends, Romans, countrymen, lend me your ears. I come to bury Caesar, not to praise him." When Caesar's body was burned, his adoring fans threw anything at hand on the fire, requiring the fire department to come put it out. Later, Emperor Augustus dedicated this temple in his name, making Caesar the first Roman to become a god.

▶ *Continue past the Temple of Julius Caesar, to the open area between the columns of the Temple of Antoninus Pius and Faustina (which we passed earlier) and the boxy brick building (the Curia). You can view these ruins of the Basilica Aemilia from a ramp next to the Temple of Antoninus Pius and Faustina, or (if the path is open) walk among them.*

⓫ Basilica Aemilia

Notice the layout. This was a long, rectangular building. The stubby columns all in a row form one long, central hall flanked by two side aisles. Medieval Christians required a larger meeting hall for their worship services than Roman temples provided, so they used the spacious Roman basilica as the model for their churches. Cathedrals from France to Spain to England, from Romanesque to Gothic to Renaissance, all have the same basic floor plan as a Roman basilica.

▶ *Now head for the big, well-preserved brick building with the triangular roof—the Curia. It's just to the right of the big triumphal arch at the foot of Capitoline Hill. While often closed, the building is impressive even from outside.*

⓬ The Curia (Senate House)

The Curia was the most important political building in the Forum. Since the birth of the republic, this was the site of Rome's official center of government. Three hundred senators, elected by the citizens of Rome, donned their togas, tucked their scrolls under their arms, and climbed the steps into this great hall.

Rome prided itself on being a republic. Early in the city's history, its people threw out the king and established rule by elected representatives. Each Roman citizen was free to speak his mind and have a say in public policy. Even when emperors became the supreme authority, the Senate was a power to be reckoned with. (Note: Although Julius Caesar was assassinated in "the Senate," it wasn't here—the Senate was temporarily meeting across town.)

The present Curia building dates from AD 283, when it replaced an earlier Senate building. It's so well preserved because it was used as a church since early Christian times. In the 1930s, it was restored as a historic site. If you have the Full Experience ticket, you can go inside the Curia.

▶ *Go back down the Senate steps and find the 10-foot-high wall just to the left of the big arch, marked...*

⓭ Rostrum

Nowhere was Roman freedom of speech more apparent than at this "Speaker's Corner." The Rostrum was a raised platform, 10 feet high and 80 feet long, decorated with statues, columns, and the prows of ships. On a stage like this, Rome's orators, great and small, tried to draw a crowd and sway public opinion. Mark Antony rose to offer Caesar the laurel-leaf crown of kingship, which Caesar publicly (and hypocritically) refused—while privately becoming a dictator.

In later years, when emperors ruled, it took real daring to speak out against the powers that be. Rome's democratic spirit was increasingly squelched. Eventually, the emperor and the army—not the Senate and the citizens—held ultimate power, and Rome's vast empire began to rot from within.

▶ *In front of the Rostrum are **trees** bearing fruits that were sacred to the ancient Romans: olives (provided food, oil for light, and preservatives), figs (tasty), and wine grapes (made a popular export product). Now turn your attention to the big arch to the right of the Rostrum, the...*

⓮ Arch of Septimius Severus

In imperial times, the Rostrum's voices of democracy would have been dwarfed by images of the empire, such as the huge six-story-high Arch of Septimius Severus (AD 203). The reliefs commemorate the African-born emperor's battles in Mesopotamia. Near ground level, see soldiers marching captured barbarians back to Rome for the victory parade. Despite efficient rule by emperors like Severus, Rome's empire began to

Arch of Septimius Severus—one of the Forum's later monuments, before Rome's long decline

crumble under the weight of its own corruption, disease, and decaying infrastructure.

▶ *As we near the end of Rome's history, we're also nearing the end of our tour. Our next stop is the Temple of Saturn. You can see it from here—it's the eight big columns just up the slope of Capitol Hill. Or you could make your way to it for a closer look.*

⓯ Temple of Saturn

These columns framed the entrance to the Forum's oldest temple (497 BC). Inside was a humble, very old wooden statue of the god Saturn. The statue's claim to fame was its pedestal, which held the gold bars, coins, and jewels of Rome's state treasury, the booty collected by conquering generals.

▶ *Now turn your attention from the Temple of Saturn, one of the Forum's first buildings, to one of its last monuments. Find a lone, tall column standing in the Forum in front of the Rostrum. It's fluted and topped with a leafy Corinthian capital. This is the...*

Remember that Rome lasted 1,000 years—500 years of growth, 200 years of peak power, and 300 years of gradual decay. The fall had many causes, among them the barbarians who pecked away at Rome's borders. Christians blamed the fall on moral decay. Pagans blamed it on Christians. Socialists blamed it on a shallow economy based on the spoils of war. (Republicans blamed it on Democrats.)

Barbarian tribes from Germany and Asia attacked the Italian peninsula and even looted Rome itself in AD 410, leveling many of the buildings in the Forum. In 476, when the last emperor checked out and switched off the lights, Europe plunged into centuries of ignorance, poverty, and weak government—the Dark Ages.

But Rome lived on in the Catholic Church. Christianity was the state religion of Rome's last generations. Emperors became popes (both called themselves "Pontifex Maximus"), senators became bishops, orators became priests, and basilicas became churches. The glory of Rome remains eternal.

⑯ Column of Phocas

This is the Forum's last monument (AD 608), a gift from the powerful Byzantine Empire to a fallen empire—Rome. Given to commemorate the pagan Pantheon's becoming a Christian church, it was a symbolic last nail in ancient Rome's coffin. After Rome's 1,000-year reign, the city was looted by Vandals, the population of a million-plus shrank to about 10,000, and the once-grand city center—the Forum—was abandoned, slowly covered up by centuries of silt and dirt. In the 1700s, an English historian named Edward Gibbon overlooked this spot from Capitoline Hill. Hearing Christian monks singing at these pagan ruins, he looked out at the few columns poking up from the ground, pondered the decline and fall of the Roman Empire, and thought, "Hmm,

Temple of Saturn—the Forum's oldest temple, on the flank of Capitoline Hill

that's a catchy title…"

▶ *Your tour is over. If you want to see Palatine Hill, don't leave the Forum complex; you won't be allowed back in without a new ticket. Instead, return to the Arch of Titus, where you can climb up to the hill (for details about this sight, see page 128). If you'd rather exit the Forum, refer to your map for possible exit locations.*

St. Peter's Basilica Tour

Basilica San Pietro

St. Peter's is the greatest church in Christendom. Its vast expanse could swallow up other churches whole. The basilica represents the power and splendor of Rome's 2,000-year domination of the Western world. Built on the memory and grave of the first pope, St. Peter, this is where the grandeur of ancient Rome became the grandeur of Christianity.

Besides sheer size, St. Peter's houses Michelangelo's dreamy *Pietà* and Bernini's towering bronze canopy. It's the place where the pope presides, and we'll catch a glimpse of the papal apartments nearby. We'll finish our visit with a sweaty climb up Michelangelo's dome for a one-of-a-kind view of Rome.

ORIENTATION

Cost: Free entry to basilica and crypt. Dome climb—€8 to only use the stairs, €10 to ride an elevator partway, then climb (cash only; see "Dome Climb," later). Treasury Museum—€5.

Hours: The **church** is open daily 7:00-19:00, Oct-March until 18:30. It closes on Wednesday mornings during papal audiences (until roughly 13:00). The **dome** (*cupola*) is open to climbers daily 7:00-17:00, last entry one hour before closing. The **Treasury Museum** is open daily 8:30-17:50. The **crypt** (*grotte*) is open daily 9:00-16:00.

Visitor Information: The shop, with an info/ticket desk, is located on the left side of the square as you face the church (Mon-Sat 8:30-18:30, closed Sun).

Planning Your Time: It makes sense to plan your visit along with the Vatican Museums (see next chapter). Consider the following time estimates: At a brisk pace, seeing St. Peter's Square takes 15 minutes; the basilica interior requires an hour (plus the line to get inside); the dome climb is an hour; and the Vatican Museums take at least 2.5 hours. Budget time for lunch and walking. From St. Peter's Square to the Vatican Museums entrance is about 15 minutes; from the Sistine Chapel to St. Peter's is about 30 minutes. The basilica can have a long security line through much of the day; it may be shorter before 9:30 and after 16:00.

Dress Code: No shorts, above-the-knee skirts, or bare shoulders. Carry a cover-up if necessary.

Getting There: Take the Metro to Ottaviano, then walk 10 minutes south on Via Ottaviano. The #40 bus drops off at Piazza Pio, next to Castel Sant'Angelo—a 10-minute walk. The more crowded bus #64 stops south of St. Peter's Square (get off after it crosses the Tiber, at the first stop past the tunnel; backtrack toward the tunnel and turn left when you see the rows of columns). Bus #492 gets you near Piazza Risorgimento (get off when you see the Vatican walls). A taxi from Termini train station costs about €15.

Church Services: Mass is generally in Italian. Confirm times on the signboard as you enter.

Tours: ∩ Download my free St. Peter's Basilica audio tour. Audioguides (likely a phone app) are €5 for the church, €15 with the dome. Ask about guided tours.

Dome Climb: The entry to the elevator is just outside the north (right) side of the basilica—look for signs to the cupola. For more on the dome, see the end of this chapter.

Length of This Tour: Allow one hour, plus another hour if you climb the dome (or a half-hour to the roof).

Baggage Check: The free bag check (mandatory for bags larger than a purse or day pack) is inside security, outside the basilica.

Other Vatican City Tours: To see the Vatican Gardens, you must book a €39 tour (several days in advance) at www.museivaticani.va. To see St. Peter's actual tomb beneath the church, book a €13 Scavi tour at least two months in advance by email (scavi@fsp.va; see instructions at www.scavi.va).

Seeing the Pope: Your best bets are on Sundays and Wednesdays. On Sunday, the pope often gives a blessing at noon (except in July and August) from an apartment overlooking St. Peter's Square. No tickets are required—just show up in the square.

On most Wednesdays at 9:30, the pope speaks to large crowds in St. Peter's Square (in winter, it's occasionally in a nearby auditorium). You can just show up and enjoy a look via jumbo-screens, but to get a seat, you'll need a (free) advance ticket. Reserve tickets (available 1-2 months in advance) by sending a request by mail or fax (access the form at Vatican.va—select "Prefecture of the Papal Household" at the bottom of the page). You'll then pick up the tickets at St. Peter's Square before the audience. Or email the Bishops' Office three months to three weeks prior to your requested date and pick up tickets the afternoon before your visit (Pnac.org, visitorsoffice@pnac.org). Alternatively, get a ticket from the usually crowded Vatican guard station on St. Peter's Square, starting the Monday before the audience.

Starring: Michelangelo, Bernini, St. Peter, a heavenly host...and, occasionally, the pope.

THE TOUR BEGINS

▶ *Find a shady spot under the columns around St. Peter's oval-shaped "square." If the pigeons left a clean spot, sit on it.*

Background

Nearly 2,000 years ago, this was the site of Nero's Circus—a huge, cigar-shaped chariot racecourse. The Romans had no marching bands, so for halftime entertainment they killed Christians. Some were crucified, some fed to lions, while others were covered in tar, tied to posts, and burned—human torches to light up the evening races.

One of those killed here, in about AD 65, was Peter, Jesus' right-hand man, who had come to Rome to spread the message of love. His remains were buried in a cemetery located where the main altar in St. Peter's is today. For 250 years, these relics were quietly and secretly revered.

When Christianity was finally legalized in 313, the Christian emperor Constantine built a church on the site of Peter's martyrdom. "Old St. Peter's" lasted 1,200 years (AD 326-1500).

By the time of the Renaissance, Old St. Peter's was falling apart and was considered unfit to be the center of the Western Church. The new, larger church we see today was begun in 1506 by the architect Donato Bramante. He was succeeded by Michelangelo and a number of other architects, each with their own designs. The church was finally finished in 1626.

St. Peter's Square

St. Peter's Square, with its ring of columns, symbolizes the arms of the church welcoming everyone—believers and nonbelievers—in its motherly embrace. It was designed a century after Michelangelo by the Baroque architect Gian Lorenzo Bernini, who did much of the work that we'll see inside. Numbers first: 284 columns, 56 feet high, in stern Doric style. Topping them are Bernini's 140 favorite saints, each 10 feet tall. The "square" itself is actually elliptical, 660 by 500 feet. It's a little higher around the edges, so that even when full of crowds, those on the periphery can see above the throngs.

The **obelisk** in the center is 90 feet of solid granite weighing more than 300 tons. Think for a second about how much history this monument has seen. Originally erected in Egypt more than 2,000 years ago, it

St. Peter's Square

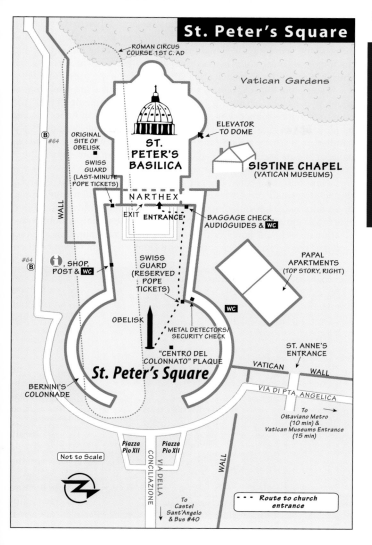

ROMAN CIRCUS COURSE 1ST C. AD

Vatican Gardens

ELEVATOR TO DOME

ORIGINAL SITE OF OBELISK

Ⓑ #64

SWISS GUARD (LAST-MINUTE POPE TICKETS)

ST. PETER'S BASILICA

SISTINE CHAPEL (VATICAN MUSEUMS)

NARTHEX

EXIT   ENTRANCE

BAGGAGE CHECK, AUDIOGUIDES & WC

WALL

#64 Ⓑ

ℹ, SHOP, POST & WC

SWISS GUARD (RESERVED POPE TICKETS)

PAPAL APARTMENTS (TOP STORY, RIGHT)

WC

OBELISK

METAL DETECTORS/ SECURITY CHECK

"CENTRO DEL COLONNATO" PLAQUE

ST. ANNE'S ENTRANCE

VATICAN   WALL

St. Peter's Square

VIA DI PTA. ANGELICA

BERNINI'S COLONNADE

To Ottaviano Metro (10 min) & Vatican Museums Entrance (15 min)

Piazza Pio XII   Piazza Pio XII

Not to Scale

VIA DELLA CONCILIAZIONE

WALL

To Castel Sant'Angelo & Bus #40

- - - Route to church entrance

witnessed the fall of the pharaohs to the Greeks and then to the Romans. Then the emperor Caligula moved it to imperial Rome, where it stood impassively watching the slaughter of Christians at the racecourse and the torture of Protestants by the Inquisition. Today, it watches over the church, a reminder that each civilization builds on the previous ones.

Facing the church, pan to the right and find the gray building at about two o'clock, rising up behind Bernini's colonnade. That's the pope's official residence. His suite of rooms is on the top floor. The last window on the right is his bedroom. To the left of that window is the window of his study. Pope Francis, however, has shunned the grand papal apartments and lives instead in a modest Vatican guesthouse. But it is from here that the pope often appears Sundays at noon.

Now find the Sistine Chapel. It's just to the right of the church's facade—the small gray-brown building with the triangular roof, topped by an antenna. That tiny pimple along the roofline midway up the left side is a chimney. That's where the famous smoke signals announce the election of each new pope. White smoke means a new pope has been selected. If the smoke is black, a two-thirds majority hasn't been reached.

St. Peter's—built on the grave of Jesus' right-hand man, and now the center of Catholicism

The papal apartments overlook the Square.

The Vatican's Swiss Guard

Walk to the right, five pavement plaques from the obelisk, to the off-center plaque marked *Centro del Colonnato*. From here, all Bernini's columns on the right side line up.

▶ *Now make your way up toward the security checkpoint. After you clear security, continue up, passing the huge statues of St. Paul (with his two-edged sword) and St. Peter (with his bushy hair and keys). Enter the church narthex.*

The Basilica

The Narthex

The narthex (portico) is itself bigger than most churches. Its huge white columns date from the first church (fourth century). Five famous bronze doors lead into the church.

Made from the melted-down bronze of the original door of Old St. Peter's, the central door is only opened on special occasions. The far-right entrance is the ❶ **Holy Door,** opened only during Holy Years (and special "Jubilee" years designated by the pope). On Christmas Eve every 25 years, the pope knocks three times with a silver hammer and the door opens, welcoming pilgrims to pass through. For Holy Year 2000, Pope John Paul II opened this door, then bricked it up again with a ceremonial trowel a year later. Although Holy Years officially come every 25 years, Pope Francis declared the year 2016 as an "Extraordinary Jubilee of Mercy" Holy Year. So, this Holy Door was once again opened. On the door itself, note the crucified Jesus and his shiny knees, polished by pious pilgrims who touch them for a blessing.

▶ *Now for one of Europe's great "wow" experiences: Enter the church.*

Gape for a while. But don't gape at Michelangelo's famous Pietà *(on the right). I'll cover it later in the tour. I'll wait for you at the round maroon pavement stone on the floor near the central doorway (#2 on the map).*

The Nave

Wow. This church is appropriately huge. Size before beauty: The golden window at the far end is two football fields away. The dove in the golden window has the wingspan of a 747 (OK, maybe not quite, but it *is* big). The church covers six acres. The lettering in the gold band along the top of the pillars is seven feet high. Really. The church has a capacity of 60,000 standing worshippers (or 1,200 tour groups).

The church is huge, but everything is designed to make it seem smaller and more intimate than it really is. For example, the statue of St. Teresa near the bottom of the first pillar on the right is 15 feet tall. The statue above her near the top looks the same size, but is actually six feet taller, giving the impression that it's not so far away. Similarly, the fancy bronze canopy over the altar at the far end is as tall as a seven-story building. That makes the great height of the dome seem smaller.

The nave of St. Peter's—two football fields long—can accommodate 60,000 worshippers.

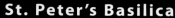

St. Peter's Basilica

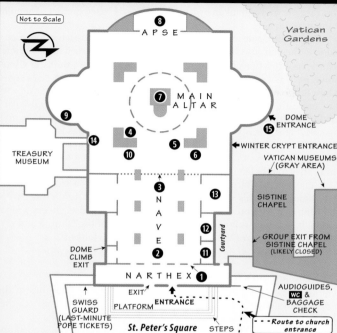

Not to Scale

APSE

Vatican Gardens

MAIN ALTAR

DOME ENTRANCE

WINTER CRYPT ENTRANCE

VATICAN MUSEUMS (GRAY AREA)

TREASURY MUSEUM

SISTINE CHAPEL

NAVE

Courtyard

GROUP EXIT FROM SISTINE CHAPEL (LIKELY CLOSED)

DOME CLIMB EXIT

NARTHEX

AUDIOGUIDES, WC & BAGGAGE CHECK

SWISS GUARD (LAST-MINUTE POPE TICKETS)

EXIT PLATFORM

ENTRANCE

St. Peter's Square

STEPS

Route to church entrance

❶ Holy Door

❷ Charlemagne's Coronation Site

❸ Michelangelo's Greek-Cross Church

❹ St. Andrew Statue; View of Dome; Crypt Entrance

❺ St. Peter Statue (with Kissable Toe)

❻ Pope John XXIII

❼ Main Altar (under Bernini's Canopy & over Peter's Tomb)

❽ BERNINI–Dove Window & Throne of St. Peter

❾ Peter's Crucifixion Site

❿ RAPHAEL–Mosaic copy of The Transfiguration

⓫ MICHELANGELO–Pietà

⓬ Tomb of Pope John Paul II

⓭ Blessed Sacrament Chapel

⓮ Treasury Museum

⓯ Dome Entrance

Looking down the nave, we get a sense of the splendor of ancient Rome that was carried on by the Catholic Church. The floor plan, with a central aisle (nave) flanked by two side aisles, is based on that of ancient Roman basilicas.

On the floor near the central doorway is a round slab of porphyry stone in the maroon color of ancient Roman officialdom. This is the spot where, on Christmas night in AD 800, the king of the Franks ❷ **Charlemagne** was crowned Holy Roman Emperor. Even in the Dark Ages, when Rome was virtually abandoned and visitors reported that the city had more thieves and wolves than decent people, its imperial legacy made it a fitting place to symbolically establish a briefly united Europe.

St. Peter's was very expensive to build. The popes financed it by selling "indulgences," allowing the rich to buy forgiveness for their sins. This kind of corruption inspired an obscure German monk named Martin Luther to rebel and start the Protestant Reformation.

The ornate, Baroque-style interior decoration—a riot of marble, gold, stucco, mosaics, columns of stone, and pillars of light—was part of the Church's "Counter" Reformation. Baroque served as cheery propaganda, impressing followers with the authority of the Church and giving them a glimpse of the heaven that awaited the faithful.

▶ *Now, walk straight up the center of the nave toward the altar.*

❸ Michelangelo's Greek-Cross Church

The plaques on the floor show where other, smaller churches of the world would end if they were placed inside St. Peter's: St. Paul's Cathedral in London (Londinense), Florence's Duomo, and so on.

You'll also walk over circular golden grates. Stop at the second one (at the third pillar from the entrance). Look back at the entrance and realize that if Michelangelo had had his way, this whole long section of the church wouldn't exist. The nave was extended after his death.

The church took 120 years to build (1506-1626). The first architect, Donato Bramante, intended the church to have four equal-length arms, radiating out from the altar in a Greek cross. But after Bramante died, the project languished for decades. Finally, Michelangelo, at age 71, was asked to take over and cap it with a dome. He agreed, intending to put the dome over Donato Bramante's original floor plan. But after Michelangelo's death, the Church, struggling against Protestants and its own corruption, opted for a floor plan designed to impress the world with its grandeur: the Latin cross of the Crucifixion.

▶ *Continue toward the altar, entering "Michelangelo's church." Park yourself in front of the* ❹ **statue of St. Andrew** *to the left of the altar. (Note that the entrance to the crypt is usually here; in winter it's by the dome entrance.)*

The Dome

The dome soars higher than a football field on end, 448 feet from the floor of the cathedral to the top of the lantern. It glows with light from its windows, the blue-and-gold mosaics creating a cool, solemn atmosphere. In this majestic vision of heaven (not painted by Michelangelo), we see (above the windows) Jesus, Mary, and a ring of saints; rings of more angels above them; and, way up in the ozone, God the Father (a blur of blue and red, unless you have binoculars).

When Michelangelo died (1564), he'd completed only the drum of the dome—the circular base up as far as the windows—but the next architects were guided by his designs.

Listen to the hum of visitors echoing through St. Peter's and reflect

Michelangelo's dome—448 feet tall—hovers directly above the altar and St. Peter's tomb.

From Pope to Pope

When a pope dies—or retires—the tiny, peaceful Vatican stirs from its timeless slumber and becomes headline news. Millions of people converge on Vatican City, and hundreds of millions around the world watch raptly on TV.

The deceased pope's body is displayed in state in front of the main altar in St. Peter's Basilica. Thousands of pilgrims line up down Via della Conciliazione, waiting for one last look at their pope. On the day of the funeral, hundreds of thousands of mourners, dignitaries, and security personnel gather in St. Peter's Square. The pope's coffin is carried out to the square, where a eulogy is given.

Most popes are laid to rest in the crypt below St. Peter's Basilica, near the tomb of St. Peter and among shrines to many other popes. Especially popular popes—such as John Paul II or John XXIII—eventually find a place upstairs, inside St. Peter's itself.

While the previous pope is being laid to rest, 100-plus cardinals, representing Catholics around the globe, descend on Rome to elect a new pope. Once they've assembled, the crimson-robed cardinals are stripped of their mobile phones, given a vow of secrecy, and locked inside the Sistine Chapel. This begins the "conclave" (from Latin *cum clave*, with key). As they cast votes, their used paper ballots are burned in a stove inside the chapel. The smoke rises up and out the tiny chimney, visible to the crowds assembled in St. Peter's Square. Black smoke means they haven't yet agreed on a new pope.

Finally, the anxious crowd looks up to see a puff of white smoke emerging from the chapel. The bells in St. Peter's clock towers ring out gloriously, the crowd erupts in cheers, and Romans watching on TV hail taxis to hurry to the square.

On the balcony outside St. Peter's, the newly elected pope steps up and raises his hands, as thousands chant "Viva il Papa." A cardinal introduces him to the crowd, announcing his newly chosen name. "Brothers and sisters," the cardinal says in several languages, *"habemus papam."* "We have a pope."

on our place in the cosmos: half animal, half angel, stretched between heaven and earth, born to live only a short while, a bubble of foam on a great cresting wave of humanity.

▶ *But I digress.*

Peter's Remains

The base of the dome is ringed with a gold banner telling us in massive blue letters why this church is so important. According to Catholics, Peter was selected by Jesus to head the church. The banner in Latin quotes from the Bible where Jesus says to him, "You are Peter *(Tu es Petrus)* and upon this rock I will build my church, and to you I will give the keys of the kingdom of heaven" (Matthew 16:18).

Peter was the first bishop of Rome. His prestige and that of the city itself made this bishopric more illustrious than all others, and Peter's authority has supposedly passed in an unbroken chain to each succeeding bishop of Rome—that is, the 260-odd popes that followed.

Under the dome, that is, under the bronze canopy, under the altar, some 23 feet under the marble floor, rest the bones of St. Peter, the "rock" upon which this particular church was built. You can't see the tomb, but you can go to the railing and look down into the small, lighted niche below the altar to see a box containing bishops' shawls—a symbol of how Peter's authority spread to other churches. Peter's tomb is just below this box.

Are the remains buried there really the bones of Jesus' apostle? According to a papal pronouncement: definitely maybe. The traditional site of his tomb was sealed when Old St. Peter's was built on it in AD 326, and it remained sealed until 1940, when it was opened for archaeological study. Bones were found, dated from the first century, of a robust

St. Andrew gazes up at the dome: "Wow!"

"Tu es Petrus"—You are Peter...

Peter, the "Fisher of Men"

According to the Bible, Peter was a fisherman chosen by Christ to catch sinners instead. This "fisher of men" had human weaknesses that have endeared him to Christians. He was the disciple who tried to walk on water—but failed. In another incident, he impetuously cut off a man's ear when soldiers came to arrest Jesus. And he even denied knowing Christ, to save his own skin. But Jesus chose him anyway and gave him his nickname—Rock (in Latin: *Petrus*).

Venerable bronze statue of Peter

Legend says that Peter came to the wicked city of Rome after Jesus' death to spread the gospel of love. He may have been imprisoned in the Mamertine Prison near the Roman Forum (see page 132), and other stories claim he had a vision of Christ along the Appian Way (described on page 158). Eventually, Peter's preaching offended the Nero administration. Christ's fisherman was arrested, crucified upside down, and buried here, where St. Peter's now stands.

man who died in old age. His body was wrapped in expensive cloth. A third-century tag artist had graffitied a wall near the tomb with "Peter is here," indicating that early visitors thought this was Peter's tomb. Does that mean it's really Peter? Who am I to disagree with the pope? Definitely maybe.

If you line up the cross on the altar with the dove in the window, you'll notice that the niche below the cross is just off-center compared with the rest of the church. Why? Because Michelangelo built the church around the traditional location of the tomb, not the actual location—about two feet away—discovered by modern archaeology.

Back in the nave—on the right side, roughly facing the crypt entrance—sits a bronze ❺ **statue of St. Peter** under a canopy. This is one of a handful of pieces of art that were in the earlier church. In one hand he holds keys, the symbol of the authority given him by Christ, while

Pope Francis I

In 2013, Cardinal Jorge Bergoglio of Argentina became Francis I, the Catholic Church's 266th pope. His election represents three "firsts": As the first pope from the Americas, Francis personifies the 80 percent of Catholics who live outside Europe. As the first Jesuit pope—from the religious order known for education—he stands for spreading the faith through teaching. And as the first Francis—named after St. Francis of Assisi—he calls to mind that medieval friar's efforts to return a corrupt church to simple Christian values of poverty and humility.

Born in 1936, Francis grew up in Buenos Aires in a family of working-class Italian immigrants. He spent his 20s in various jobs (chemist, high-school teacher) before entering the priesthood and eventually becoming archbishop of Buenos Aires.

Francis lives simply, staying in a Vatican guesthouse rather than the official papal apartments. He reportedly eats leftovers. When people talk about Francis, the word that comes up is often "dialogue." He's known for listening to every point of view, whether mediating between dictators and union leaders, sitting down with the Orthodox Patriarch, celebrating Rosh Hashanah with Jews, visiting a mosque, or speaking well of gay people and atheists. He speaks a number of languages, including fluent Italian—the language of his parents and of the Vatican.

Francis inherited a Catholic Church with many problems: financial shenanigans, charges that they've protected pedophiles, and alleged blackmailing of gay priests. But Francis is also a strong defender of traditional Catholic beliefs. No one expects major shifts under Francis in the Church's positions on abortion, gay marriage, contraception, or the celibate, male-only priesthood.

As pope, Francis has made it clear that he wants the Church to focus less on money and power, and more on the poor and the outcast. One of his favorite Christian rituals is to literally kneel down before the poor, sick, or imprisoned, and wash their feet. Francis' personal credo, *"Miserando atque elignedo,"* focuses on how God shows "mercy"—*miserando*—and compassion by forgiving sinners and helping the downtrodden.

with the other hand he blesses us. He's wearing the toga of a Roman senator. It may be that the original statue was of a senator and that the bushy head and keys were added later to make it Peter. His big right toe has been worn smooth by the lips of pilgrims and foot fetishists. If the statue is accessible, stand in line and kiss it, or, to avoid foot-and-mouth disease, touch your hand to your lips, then rub the toe. This is simply an act of reverence with no legend attached, though you can make one up if you like.

▶ *Circle to the right around the statue of Peter to find another stop that's popular among pilgrims: the lighted glass niche with the red-robed body of ❻ Pope John XXIII (reigned 1958-1963). Now known as Saint John, it was he who initiated the landmark Vatican II Council (1962-1965) that instituted major reforms, bringing the Church into the modern age.*

❼ The Main Altar

The main altar (the white marble slab with cross and candlesticks) beneath the dome and canopy is used only when the pope himself says Mass. He sometimes conducts the Sunday morning service when he's in town, a sight worth seeing. I must admit, though, it's a little strange being frisked for weapons at the door to the holiest place in Christendom.

The tiny altar would be lost in this enormous church if it weren't for Gian Lorenzo Bernini's seven-story bronze canopy (God's "four-poster bed"), which "extends" the altar upward and reduces the perceived distance between floor and ceiling. The corkscrew columns echo the marble ones that surrounded the altar/tomb in Old St. Peter's. Some of the bronze used here was taken and melted down from the ancient Pantheon.

Bernini (1598-1680), the Michelangelo of the Baroque era, is the man most responsible for the interior decoration of the church. As an architect, sculptor, and painter, Bernini was uniquely qualified to turn St. Peter's into a multimedia extravaganza. Nowhere is there such a conglomeration of works by the flamboyant genius who remade the church—and the city—in the Baroque style.

The altar area was his masterpiece, a "theater" for holy spectacles. Besides the bronze canopy, Bernini did the statue of lance-bearing St. Longinus ("The hills are alive..."), the balconies above the four statues, and much of the marble floor decoration. Bernini gave an impressive unity to an amazing variety of pillars, windows, statues, chapels, and aisles.

▶ *Approach the apse, the front area with the golden dove window.*

Bernini's bronze canopy rises above the main altar, creating a proscenium for the Mass.

The Apse

Bernini's ❽ **dove window** shines above the smaller front altar used for everyday services. The Holy Spirit, in the form of a six-foot-high dove, pours sunlight onto the faithful through the alabaster windows, turning into artificial rays of gold and reflecting off swirling gold clouds, angels, and winged babies. During a service, real sunlight passes through real clouds of incense, mingling with Bernini's sculpture. This is the epitome of Baroque—an ornate, mixed-media work designed to overwhelm the viewer.

Beneath the dove is the centerpiece of this structure, the so-called **Throne of St. Peter,** an oak chair built in medieval times for a king. Subsequently, it was encrusted with tradition and encased in bronze by Bernini as a symbol of papal authority. Statues of four early Church Fathers support the chair, a symbol of how bishops should support the pope in troubled times—like the Counter-Reformation.

Remember that St. Peter's is a church, not a museum. In the apse, Mass is said daily for pilgrims, tourists, and Roman citizens alike. Wooden booths are available for Catholics to confess their sins to a listening ear and receive forgiveness and peace of mind. The faithful renew their faith, and the faithless gain inspiration. Look at the light streaming through the windows, turn and gaze up into the dome, and quietly contemplate your deity (or lack thereof).

▶ *To the left of the main altar is the south transept. It may be roped off for worship, but anyone can step past the guard if you say you're there "for prayer." At the far end, left side, find the dark "painting" of St. Peter crucified upside down.*

The dove window designed by Bernini

Sunbeams often light the afternoon service.

❾ Peter's Crucifixion Site

This marks the exact spot (according to tradition) where Peter was killed 1,900 years ago. Peter had come to the world's greatest city to preach Jesus' message of love to the pagan, often hostile Romans. During the reign of Emperor Nero, he was arrested and brought to Nero's Circus so all of Rome could witness his execution. When the authorities told Peter he was to be crucified just like his Lord, Peter said, essentially, "I'm not worthy" and insisted they nail him on the cross upside down.

The Romans were actually quite tolerant of other religions, but they required their conquered peoples to worship the Roman emperor as a god. But monotheistic Christians refused to worship the emperor even when they were burned alive, crucified, or thrown to the lions. Their bravery, optimism in suffering, and message of love struck a chord among slaves and members of the lower classes. The religion started by a poor carpenter grew, despite the occasional persecution of minorities by fanatical emperors. In three short centuries, Christianity went from a small Jewish sect in Jerusalem to the official religion of the world's greatest empire.

Around the corner on the right (heading back toward the central nave), pause at the mosaic copy of Raphael's epic painting of ❿ *The Transfiguration.* The original is now beautifully displayed in the Pinacoteca of the Vatican Museums.

▶ *Back near the entrance of the church, in the far corner, behind bulletproof glass, is the sculpture everyone has come to see, the...*

⓫ *Pietà*

Michelangelo was 24 years old when he completed this *pietà*—a representation of Mary with the body of Christ taken from the cross. It was Michelangelo's first major commission (by the French ambassador to the Vatican), done for Holy Year 1500.

In Italian, *pietà* means "pity." Michelangelo, with his total mastery of the real world, captures the sadness of the moment. Mary cradles her crucified son in her lap. Christ's lifeless right arm drooping down lets us know how heavy this corpse is. His smooth skin is accented by the rough folds of Mary's robe. Mary tilts her head down, looking at her dead son with sad tenderness. Her left hand turns upward, asking, "How could they do this to you?"

Michelangelo didn't think of sculpting as creating a figure, but as simply freeing the God-made figure from the prison of marble around it. He'd attack a project like this with an inspired passion, chipping away to find what God had placed inside.

The bunched-up shoulder and rigor-mortis legs show that Michelangelo learned well from his studies of cadavers. But realistic as this work is, its true power lies in the subtle "unreal" features. Life-size Christ looks childlike compared with larger-than-life Mary, which accentuates the impression of Mary enfolding Jesus in her maternal love. Mary—the mother of a 33-year-old man—looks like a teenager, emphasizing how she was the eternally youthful "handmaiden" of the Lord, always serving God's will, even if it means giving up her son.

The statue is a solid pyramid of maternal tenderness. Yet within this, Christ's body tilts diagonally down to the right and Mary's hem flows with it. Subconsciously, we feel the weight of this dead God sliding from her lap to the ground.

In 1972, a madman with a hammer entered St. Peter's and began hacking away at the *Pietà*. The damage was repaired, but there's now a shield of bulletproof glass in front of the sculpture.

The *Pieta*, by 24-year-old Michelangelo, was one of the rare statues he polished to perfection.

This is Michelangelo's only signed work. The story goes that he overheard some pilgrims praising his finished *Pietà,* but attributing it to a second-rate sculptor from a lesser city. He was so enraged that he grabbed his chisel and chipped "Michelangelo Buonarroti of Florence did this" in the ribbon running down Mary's chest.

On your right (covered in gray concrete with a gold cross) is the back side of the Holy Door. It will be opened in 2025, the next Jubilee Year. If there's a prayer inside you, ask that St. Peter's will no longer need security checks or bulletproof glass when this door is next opened.

▶ *In the chapel to the left is …*

The Rest of the Church

⑫ **Tomb of Pope John Paul II** (Chapel of San Sebastian): The tomb of Pope John Paul II (1920-2005) was moved to the chapel of San Sebastian in 2011, after he was beatified by Pope Benedict XVI. Now Saint John Paul, he lies beneath a painting of his favorite saint, the steadfast St. Sebastian.

Crypt (a.k.a. Grotte, or Tombe): The entrance to the church's "basement" is usually beside the statue of St. Andrew, to the left of the main altar (#4 on the map). You descend to the floor level of Old St. Peter's, and see tombs of popes, including Paul VI (1897-1978), who suffered reluctantly through the church's modernization. The finale is the unimpressive "sepulcher of Peter." This lighted niche with an icon is not Peter's actual tomb, but part of a shrine that stands atop Peter's tomb. The walk through the crypt is free and quick (15 minutes), but you won't see St. Peter's original grave unless you take a *Scavi* (excavations) tour. You'll end up, usually, near the cloakroom, or possibly outside.

⑬ **Blessed Sacrament Chapel:** Worshippers are welcome to step through the metalwork gates into this oasis of peace located on the right-hand side of the church, about midway to the altar.

⑭ **Treasury Museum** (Museo-Tesoro): The museum, on the left side of the nave near the altar, contains the room-size tomb of Sixtus IV by Antonio Pollaiuolo, a big pair of Roman pincers used to torture Christians, an original corkscrew column from Old St. Peter's, and assorted jewels, papal robes, and golden reliquaries—a marked contrast to the poverty of early Christians.

Vatican City

The tiny independent country of Vatican City is contained entirely within Rome. (Its 100 acres could fit eight times over in New York's Central Park.) The Vatican has its own postal system, armed guards, beautiful gardens, helipad, mini train station, radio station (KPOP), and euro coin (with a portrait of the pope). Politically powerful, the Vatican is the religious capital of 1.3 billion Roman Catholics. If you're not a Catholic, become one for your visit.

The pope is both the religious and secular leader of Vatican City. For centuries, the Vatican was the capital of the Papal States, and locals referred to the pontiff as "King Pope." Because of the Vatican's territorial ambitions, it didn't always have good relations with Italy. Although modern Italy was created in 1870, the Holy See didn't recognize it as a country until 1929.

Dome (Cupola)

A good way to finish a visit to St. Peter's is to go up to the dome for the best view of Rome anywhere. The ⓯ **entrance to the dome** is along the right (north) side of the church, but the line begins to form out front, at the church's right door (as you face the church). Look for *cupola* signs.

There are two levels: the rooftop of the church and the very top of the dome. Climb or take an elevator to the first level, on the church roof just above the facade. From the roof, you have a commanding view of St. Peter's Square, the statues on the colonnade, Rome across the Tiber in front of you, and the dome itself—almost terrifying in its nearness—looming behind you. (Depending on the routing when you visit, you might see this view from the roof only after descending from the dome.)

From the roof, you can also go inside the gallery ringing the interior of the dome and look down inside the church. Notice the dusty top of Bernini's seven-story-tall canopy far below. Study the mosaics up close—and those huge letters!

From this level, if you're energetic, continue all the way up to the top of the dome. The staircase actually winds between the outer shell and the inner one. It's a sweaty, crowded, claustrophobic 15-minute, 323-step climb, but worth it. The view from the summit is great, the fresh air even better.

It's a sweaty 323-step climb to the top of the dome, but the view is heavenly.

Admire the arms of Bernini's colonnade encircling St. Peter's Square. Find the big, white Victor Emmanuel Monument, with the two statues on top; and the Pantheon, with its large, light, shallow dome. Look down into the square at the tiny pilgrims buzzing like electrons around the nucleus of Catholicism.

Vatican Museums Tour

Musei Vaticani

The glories of the ancient world are on display in this lavish papal palace. Start with ancient Egyptian mummies and some of the best Greek and Roman statues in captivity. Then traverse long halls lined with old maps, tapestries, fig leaves, and broken penises. Pass through the popes' former home, where the painter Raphael boldly celebrated pagan philosophers in the heart of Christendom. Our visit culminates with Michelangelo's glorious Sistine Chapel, which has a centerpiece that shows God reaching out to pass the divine spark of life to man.

It's inspiring...and exhausting. But with this chapter as your guide, you'll easily sweep through 5,000 years of human history.

ORIENTATION

Cost: €21, price includes €4 online reservation fee, free on the last Sun of each month (when it's very crowded).

Hours: Mon-Sat 9:00-18:00 (Fri-Sat until 22:30 late April-Oct), closed Sun—except last Sun of month, when it's open 9:00-14:00. Guards start ushering people out of the museum 30 minutes before the official closing time. The museum is closed about a dozen days a year for religious holidays. Confirm latest opening hours on the museum website.

Information: +39 06 6988 4676, www.museivaticani.va.

Advance Reservations: The Vatican Museums can be extremely crowded, with waits of up to two hours just to buy tickets. Bypass these long lines by reserving an entry time at their website. For this chapter's sights, select the ticket called "Vatican Museums and Sistine Chapel." You'll receive a QR code via email; show the code to get a paper ticket when you arrive. (You can also print out the attached voucher—but you'll still have to swap it for a paper ticket.)

If you didn't get tickets in advance, consider booking a guided tour (see "Tours," next page) or buy same-day timed-entry tickets either on your phone, at the shop in St. Peter's Square (see previous chapter), or at the Opera Romana Pellegrinaggi, a private pilgrimage tour company (€30, office in front of St. Peter's Square, Piazza Pio XII 9).

Planning Your Time: The Vatican Museums are generally packed for much of the day. In general, the best time to visit is a weekday after 14:00 (the later, the better). The worst days are Saturdays, the last Sunday of the month (a free-entry day), Mondays, rainy days, and

Vatican Museums entrance

Modern sphere in a Renaissance courtyard

any day before or after a holiday closure. A good time to visit can be Wednesday mornings, when most tourists are at St. Peter's attending the papal audience.

One smart plan is to reserve the museums for after lunch (around 13:00), as crowds start to slightly thin out. Tour the museums, then walk to the basilica as that line begins to wane. With this plan, you'll have to move briskly to fit everything in before closing (check the dome climb's last entry hours, as you may need to do this before touring the basilica).

Dress Code: Modest dress is required (no shorts, above-knee skirts, or bare shoulders).

Getting There: The Ottaviano Metro stop is a 10-minute walk from the entrance. Buses #49, #23, and #492 stop nearby. Bus #64 stops on the other side of St. Peter's Square, a 15- to 20-minute walk. Or take a taxi from the city center.

Getting In: Approaching the exterior entrance (the big white door), you'll see three lines: individuals without reservations (far left), individuals with reservations (usually shorter and faster), and groups (on the right). All visitors must pass through a metal detector.

Tours: A €7 audioguide is available at the top of the spiral ramp/escalator (confirm the drop-off location when renting) or 🎧 download my free Vatican Museums and Sistine Chapel audio tours. The Vatican offers guided tours in English (€34, includes admission, book online).

Length of This Tour: 2.5 hours.

Services: The museum's "checkroom" (to the right after security) takes only bigger bags, not day bags.

Cuisine Art: A $ self-service cafeteria is inside, downstairs, near the Pinacoteca. Smaller $$ cafés are in the outdoor Pinecone Courtyard (Cortile della Pigna) and near the Sistine Chapel. For nearby restaurant recommendations, see page 192.

Starring: World history, a pope's palace, Michelangelo, Raphael, *Laocoön,* the Greek masters, and their Roman copyists.

THE TOUR BEGINS

This heavyweight museum is shaped like a barbell—two buildings connected by a long hall. The entrance building covers the ancient world (Egypt, Greece, Rome). The building at the far end covers its "rebirth" in the Renaissance (including the Sistine Chapel). The halls there and back are a mix of old and new. Move quickly—don't burn out before the

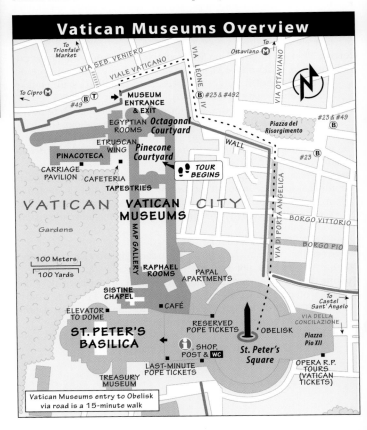

Vatican Museums Overview

Sistine Chapel at the end—and see how each civilization borrows from and builds upon the previous one.

▶ *Our tour starts in the Vatican Museums' large open-air courtyard called the "Pinecone Courtyard" (Cortile della Pigna). To get there, take the long escalator or spiral ramp up, up, up to a glass-covered patio. Go left, and after 50 yards you'll emerge into the open air of the...*

Pinecone Courtyard

Locate the big bronze ball in the center of the courtyard, and the 12-foot-tall pinecone. This vast space is the perfect place to start your visit of this vast museum. The Pinecone Courtyard sums up the Vatican's entire collection: Pinecone—ancient. Bronze sphere—modern. And the courtyard around it—Renaissance, designed by Bramante.

▶ *We start with the Egyptian collection. To get there, face the pinecone and turn left, backtracking through the door you just came through. Immediately after the doorway, turn right up a flight of marble stairs to reach the first-floor Egyptian rooms. Enter, and don't stop until you find your mummy.*

    Note: Occasionally, the stairs up to Egypt are closed off. If so, just follow the masses until you reach the Octagonal Courtyard with the Apollo Belvedere and Laocoön figures. Tour the museum from there to the "Sarcophagi," where you'll find the entrance to the Egyptian rooms.

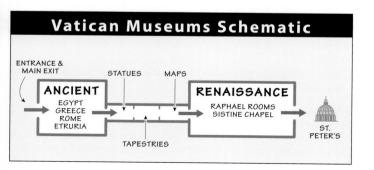

Vatican Museums Schematic

ENTRANCE & MAIN EXIT

STATUES   MAPS

ANCIENT
EGYPT
GREECE
ROME
ETRURIA

RENAISSANCE
RAPHAEL ROOMS
SISTINE CHAPEL

ST. PETER'S

TAPESTRIES

ANCIENT WING

Egypt (3000-1000 BC)

Egyptian art was religious, not decorative. A statue or painting preserved the likeness of someone, giving them a form of eternal life. Most of the art was for tombs, where they put the mummies.

▶ *Pass beyond the imitation Egyptian pillars into the second room. Go to the far end of the big glass case in the middle of this room, and find...*

❶ Mummies

This woman died three millennia ago. Her corpse was disemboweled, and her organs were placed in a jar like those you see nearby. Then the body was refilled with pitch, dried with natron (a natural sodium carbonate), wrapped in linen, and placed in a wood coffin, which went inside a stone coffin, which was then placed inside a tomb. Notice the henna job on her hair—in the next life, your spirit needed a body to be rooted to...and you wanted to look your best.

Painted inside the coffin lid is a list of what the deceased "packed" for the journey to eternity. The coffins were decorated with magical spells to protect the body from evil and to act as crib notes for the confused soul in the netherworld.

▶ *In the next room are...*

❷ Egyptian Statues

Egyptian statues walk awkwardly, as if they're carrying heavy buckets, with arms straight down at their sides. Even these Roman reproductions (made for Hadrian's Villa) are stiff, two-dimensional, and schematic—the art is only realistic enough to get the job done. In Egyptian belief, a statue like this could be a stable refuge for the wandering soul of a dead person. Each was made according to an established set of proportions.

▶ *Walk through the next small room and into the curved hallway, and look for...*

❸ Various Egyptian Gods as Animals

Before technology made humans top dogs on earth, it was easier to appreciate our fellow creatures. Egyptians saw the superiority of animals and worshipped them as incarnations of the gods. Wander through a

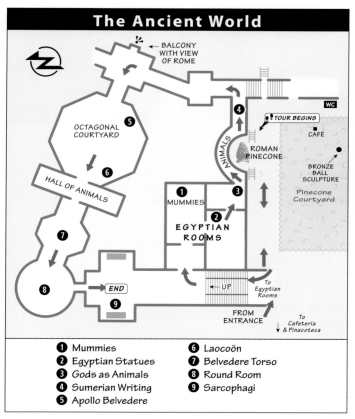

The Ancient World

BALCONY WITH VIEW OF ROME

OCTAGONAL COURTYARD

HALL OF ANIMALS

MUMMIES

EGYPTIAN ROOMS

ANIMALS

ROMAN PINECONE

TOUR BEGINS

WC

CAFÉ

BRONZE BALL SCULPTURE

Pinecone Courtyard

END

UP

To Egyptian Rooms

FROM ENTRANCE

To Cafeteria & Pinacoteca

❶ Mummies
❷ Egyptian Statues
❸ Gods as Animals
❹ Sumerian Writing
❺ Apollo Belvedere
❻ Laocoön
❼ Belvedere Torso
❽ Round Room
❾ Sarcophagi

pet store of Egyptian animal gods. Find Anubis, a jackal in a toga. In the curved room, find the lioness, the fierce goddess Sekhmet. The clever baboon is the god of wisdom, Thoth. At the end of the curved hall on your right is Bes (the small white marble statue), the patron of pregnant women (and beer-bellied men).

▶ *Continue to the third room (Room VIII), pausing at the glass case, which contains small, brown clay tablets.*

Anubis—a jackal in a toga

Sumerian writing on clay tablets

❹ Sumerian Writing

Even before Egypt, civilizations flourished in the Middle East. The Sumerian culture in Mesopotamia (the ancestors of the ancient Babylonians and of today's Iraqis) invented writing in about 3000 BC. People wrote on clay tablets by pressing into the wet clay with a wedge-shaped (cuneiform) pen. The Sumerians also rolled cylindrical seals into soft clay to make an impression that authenticated documents and marked property.

▶ *Pass through the next room, and then turn left, to a balcony with a view of Rome through the window. Then enter the Octagonal Courtyard.*

Greek and Roman Sculpture (500 BC–AD 500)

This palace wouldn't be here, all this sculpture wouldn't be here, and our lives would likely be quite different if it weren't for a few thousand Greeks in a small city about 450 years before Christ. Athens set the tone for the rest of the West. Democracy, theater, economics, literature, and art all flourished in Athens during a 50-year golden age. Greek culture was then appropriated by Rome, and revived again 1,500 years later, during the Renaissance. The Renaissance popes built and decorated these papal palaces, re-creating the glory of the classical world.

▶ *Find the statue of* Apollo Belvedere, *on your left as you enter.*

❺ *Apollo Belvedere*

Apollo, the god of the sun and of music, is hunting. He's been running through the woods, and now he spots his prey. Keeping his eye on the animal, he slows down and prepares to put a (missing) arrow into his

Apollo Belvedere—a god in human form

"Snakes! Why did it have to be snakes?"

(missing) bow. The optimistic Greeks conceived of their gods in human form...and buck naked.

This Roman copy (2nd century AD) of a Hellenistic original followed the style of the great Greek sculptor Praxiteles. It fully captures the beauty of the human form. The anatomy is perfect, and his pose is natural. Instead of standing at attention, face-forward with his arms at his sides (Egyptian-style), Apollo is on the move, coming to rest with his weight on one leg.

The Greeks loved balance. A well-rounded man was both a thinker and an athlete, a poet and a warrior. In art, the *Apollo Belvedere* balances several opposites. He's moving, but not out of control. Apollo eyes his target, but hasn't attacked yet. He's realistic, but with idealized, godlike features. The only sour note: his left hand, added in modern times. Could we try a size smaller?

▶ *In the neighboring niche to the right, a bearded old Roman river god lounges in the shade. His pose inspired Michelangelo's Adam, in the Sistine Chapel (coming up later). In the next niche is...*

❻ *Laocoön*

Laocoön (lay-AWK-oh-wahn), the high priest of Troy, had warned his fellow Trojans: "Beware of Greeks bearing gifts." The attacking Greeks had brought the Trojan Horse to the gates as a ploy to get inside the city walls, and Laocoön tried to warn his people not to bring it inside. But the gods wanted the Greeks to win, so they sent huge snakes to crush Laocoön and his two sons to death. We see them at the height of their terror, when they realize that, no matter how hard they struggle, they— and their entire race—are doomed.

The figures (carved from four blocks of marble pieced together seamlessly) are powerful, not light and graceful. The poses are as twisted as possible, accentuating every rippling muscle and bulging vein.

Laocoön was sculpted some four centuries after the golden age (5th-4th century BC), after the scales of "balance" had been tipped. *Apollo* is serene, graceful, and godlike, while *Laocoön* is powerful, emotional, and gritty.

Laocoön—the most famous Greek statue in ancient Rome—was lost for more than a thousand years. Then, in 1506, it was unexpectedly unearthed near the Colosseum. It was cleaned off and paraded through the streets in front of an awestruck populace. No one had ever seen anything like its motion and emotion. One of those who saw it was the young Michelangelo, and it was a revelation to him. Two years later, he started work on the Sistine Chapel, and the Renaissance was about to take another turn.

▶ *Leave the courtyard to the right of* Laocoön *and pause at the Hall of Animals (on the left), a Hellenistic zoo of beasts real and surreal. Then continue to the limbless torso in the middle of the next large hall.*

❼ Belvedere Torso

This hunk of shaped rock makes you appreciate the sheer physical labor involved in chipping a figure out of solid stone. It takes great strength but, at the same time, great delicacy.

This is all that remains of an ancient statue damaged by time. It shows a powerful man seated on an animal skin. Maybe it's Hercules with his lion skin, maybe a Cyclops—no one's quite sure.

Michelangelo loved this old rock. He'd caress this statue lovingly and tell people, "I am the pupil of the Torso." To him, it contained all the

Belvedere Torso—ugly beauty

Everything's bigger in ancient Rome.

beauty of classical sculpture. But it's not beautiful. Compared with the pure grace of the *Apollo*, it's downright ugly.

But Michelangelo, an ugly man himself, was looking for a new kind of beauty—not the beauty of idealized gods, but the innate beauty of every person, even so-called ugly ones. With its knotty lumps of muscle, the Torso has a brute power and a distinct personality despite—or because of—its rough edges.

▶ *Now, enter the next, domed room.*

❽ Round Room

This room, modeled on the Pantheon interior, gives some idea of Roman grandeur. Romans took Greek ideas and made them bigger, like the big bronze statue of Hercules with his club. The mosaic floor once decorated the bottom of a pool in an ancient Roman bath. The enormous Roman basin/hot tub/birdbath/vase decorated Nero's place. It was made of a single block of purple porphyry marble stone imported from Egypt. (It's so big that this 18th-century room was built around it.) Purple was a rare, royal, expensive, and prestigious color in pre-Crayola days. This particular variety was the stone of emperors...and then of popes.

▶ *Enter the next room.*

❾ Sarcophagi

These two large porphyry marble coffins were made (though not used) for the Roman emperor Constantine's mother (Helena, on left) and daughter (Constanza, on right). Both sarcophagi were quarried and worked in Egypt. The technique for working this extremely hard stone (a special tempering of metal was required) was lost after this, and porphyry marble was not chiseled again until Renaissance times.

▶ *To continue our tour, go upstairs. You'll find yourself at the head of a long hallway lined with statues.*

The Long March

```
                    DIANA THE
                    HUNTRESS   BACCHUS                          RAPHAEL
                                                               ROOMS
    ANCIENT       ■    ■
    WORLD
                 CANDELABRA    TAPESTRIES   MAPS
                      ⑩            ⑪        ⑫            &

                 ■                                          SISTINE
    ARTEMIS                      VIEW OF  ↗               CHAPEL
                                ST. PETER'S DOME

              ◄───────  APPROX. 1/4 MILE  ───────►
```

The Long March—Sculpture, Tapestries, Maps, and Views

This quarter-mile walk gives you a sense of the scale that Renaissance popes built on. The popes loved beautiful things—statues, urns, marble floors, friezes, stuccoed ceilings—and, as heirs of imperial Rome, they felt they deserved such luxury. It was extravagant spending like this that inspired Martin Luther to rebel, starting the Protestant Reformation.

⑩ Gallery of the Candelabra: Classical Sculpture

About 30 yards along the long hall, stop at the statue of **Diana,** the virgin goddess of the hunt. Roman hunters would pray and give offerings to statues like this to get divine help in their search for food.

Farmers might pray to another version of the same goddess, in her guise as **Artemis,** on the opposite wall. This billion-breasted beauty stood for fertility. "Boobs or bulls' balls?" Some historians say that bulls were sacrificed and castrated, with the testicles draped over the statues as symbols of fertility.

Shuffle along another 30 yards. On the left is **Bacchus,** with a baby on his shoulders. Many of these statues originally looked much different than they do now. First, they were painted, often in gaudy colors. Bacchus may have had brown hair, rosy cheeks, purple grapes, and a leopard-skin sidekick at his feet. Even the Apollo Belvedere, whose cool gray tones we now admire as "classic Greek austerity," may have had a paisley pink cloak for all we know. Also, many statues had glass eyes like Bacchus'.

And the fig leaves? Those came from the years 1550 to 1800, when the Church decided that certain parts of the human anatomy were ob-

Artemis—Boobs or bulls' balls?

Tapestries are remarkable for their realism.

scene. (Why not the feet?) Perhaps Church leaders associated these full-frontal statues with the outbreak of Renaissance humanism that reduced their power in Europe. Whatever the cause, they reacted by covering classical crotches with plaster fig leaves, the same leaves Adam and Eve had used when the concept of "privates" was invented.

▶ *Cover your eyes in case they forgot a fig leaf or two, and continue to the...*

⑪ Tapestries

Along the left wall are tapestries designed by Raphael's workshop and made in Brussels. They show scenes from the life of Christ: Baby Jesus in the manger, being adored by shepherds, and so on. About two-thirds of the way down the hall, find the Resurrection tapestry (on the left), with Jesus striding out of the tomb. It's curiously interactive...as you walk, Jesus' eyes, feet, knee, and even the stone slab seem to follow you across the room.

▶ *At the end of the hall, enter the...*

⑫ Map Gallery (with View of Vatican City)

This jaw-dropping gallery is the best place to appreciate the splendor of what this museum once was—the popes' palace. The crusted ceiling is pure papal splendor. The maps on the walls show the regions of Italy— "Sicilia," "Sardinia," and so on. Popes could take visitors on a tour of Italy, from the toe (entrance end) to the Alps (far end).

Glance out the windows. This is your best look at the tiny country of Vatican City, officially established as an independent nation in 1929. What you see here is pretty much all there is—these gardens, the palaces you're in, and St. Peter's.

The Map Gallery gives a glimpse of the former luxury of the palace of the popes.

▶ *Exit the map room. You may have to choose between two routes. One makes a beeline to the Sistine Chapel. But for our tour, turn left, toward the "Stanze di Raffaello"—the exquisite Raphael Rooms.*

RENAISSANCE WING

Raphael Rooms

We've seen art from the ancient world; now we'll see its rebirth in the Renaissance. We're entering the living quarters of the great Renaissance popes—where they slept, worked, and worshipped. They hired the best artists—mostly from Florence—to paint the walls and ceilings, combining classical and Christian motifs.

Entering, you'll immediately see a huge 19th-century painting of the **⑬ liberation of Vienna.** This is not by Raphael, but by Jan Matejko, a Polish painter who specialized in grand-scale historical epics like this one.

The second room's non-Raphael paintings commemorate the doctrine of the **⑭ Immaculate Conception,** establishing that Mary herself was born without sin. In the center, the pope rises to proclaim the new doctrine. Notice how his inspiration comes straight from heaven: From the upper-left corner of the painting, a thin ray of light beams directly down onto the pope.

▶ *Next, you'll pass along an outside walkway that overlooks a courtyard, finally ending up in the first of the Raphael Rooms, the...*

⓮ Constantine Room

These frescoes, painted between 1517 and 1524 (finished after Raphael's death by his assistants), celebrate the passing of the baton from one culture to the next. On the night of October 27, AD 312 (left wall), as General Constantine (in gold, with crown) was preparing his troops for a coup d'état, he saw something strange. A cross appeared in the sky with the words, "You will conquer in this sign."

The next day (long wall), his troops raged victoriously into battle with the Christian cross atop their Roman eagle banners. Constantine even stripped (right wall) and knelt before the pope to be baptized a Christian (some say). As emperor, he legalized Christianity and worked

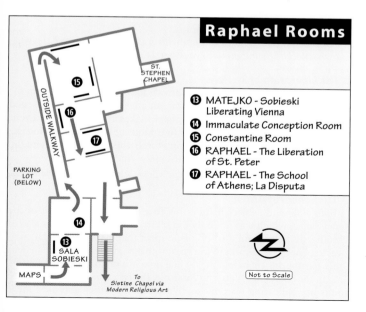

Raphael Rooms

ST. STEPHEN CHAPEL

OUTSIDE WALKWAY

PARKING LOT (BELOW)

MAPS

SALA SOBIESKI

To Sistine Chapel via Modern Religious Art

⓭ MATEJKO - Sobieski Liberating Vienna
⓮ Immaculate Conception Room
⓯ Constantine Room
⓰ RAPHAEL - The Liberation of St. Peter
⓱ RAPHAEL - The School of Athens; La Disputa

Not to Scale

Raphael (1483-1520)

Raphael was only 25 when Pope Julius II invited him, in 1508, to paint the walls of his personal living quarters. Julius was so impressed by Raphael's talent that he had the work of earlier masters scraped off and gave Raphael free rein to paint what he wanted.

Raphael lived a charmed life. He was handsome and sophisticated, and soon became Julius' favorite. He painted masterpieces effortlessly. In a different decade, he might have been thrown out of the Church as a great sinner, but his love affairs and devil-may-care personality seemed to epitomize the optimistic pagan spirit of the Renaissance.

Raphael's paintings are bathed in an even light, with few shadows; his brushwork is smooth and blended, and colors are restrained. While always graceful, his works are never lightweight or frilly—they're strong, balanced, and harmonious in the best Renaissance tradition. When he died, at just 37 years old, the High Renaissance died with him.

hand in hand with the pope.

▶ *Continue on. You'll reach a room with frescoes arching over the windows. Block the sunlight with your hand to see...*

⑯ *The Liberation of St. Peter*

Peter, Jesus' right-hand man, was thrown into prison in Jerusalem for his beliefs. In the middle of the night, an angel appeared and rescued him from the sleeping guards. Raphael makes the miraculous event even more dramatic with the use of four kinds of light illuminating the dark cell—half-moonlight, the captain's torch, the radiant angel, and the natural light spilling through the museum's window.

▶ *Enter the next room. Here in the pope's private study, Raphael painted...*

⑰ *The School of Athens*

In both style and subject matter, this fresco sums up the spirit of the Renaissance, which was not only the rebirth of classical art, but also of learning, discovery, and the optimistic spirit that man is a rational creature. Raphael pays respect to the great thinkers and scientists of ancient Greece, gathering them together at one time in a mythical school setting.

In the center are Plato and Aristotle, the two greatest Greeks. Plato points up, indicating his philosophy that mathematics and pure ideas

The School of Athens—ancient philosophers with contemporary faces, including Michelangelo's

are the source of truth, while Aristotle gestures down, showing preference for hands-on study of the material world. There's their master, Socrates (midway to the left, in green), ticking off arguments on his fingers. And in the foreground at right, bald Euclid bends over a slate to demonstrate a geometrical formula.

Raphael shows that Renaissance thinkers were as good as the ancients. There's Leonardo da Vinci, whom Raphael worshipped, in the role of Plato. Euclid is the architect Donato Bramante, who designed St. Peter's. Raphael himself (next to last on the far right, with the black beret) looks out at us. And the "school" building is actually an early version of St. Peter's Basilica (under construction at the time).

Raphael balances everything symmetrically—thinkers to the left, scientists to the right, with Plato and Aristotle dead center—showing the geometrical order found in the world. Look at the square floor tiles in the foreground. If you laid a ruler over them and extended the line upward, it would run right to the center of the picture. Similarly, the tops of the columns all point down to the middle. All the lines of sight draw our attention to Plato and Aristotle, and to the small arch over their heads—a halo over these two secular saints in the divine pursuit of knowledge.

While Raphael was painting this room, Michelangelo was at work down the hall in the Sistine Chapel. Raphael had just finished *The*

School of Athens when he got a look at Michelangelo's powerful figures and dramatic scenes. He was astonished. From this point on, Raphael began to beef up his delicate, graceful style to a more heroic level. He returned to *The School of Athens* and added one more figure to the scene—Michelangelo, the brooding, melancholy figure in front, leaning on a block of marble.

On the opposite wall Raphael's *La Disputa* portrays how grace descends from Christ (at top) via the Holy Spirit (the dove, in the center) into the Communion wafer (on the altar below).

▶ *Exit the final Raphael Room through a passageway, bear right, and go down the stairs. At the foot of the stairs you'll find several quiet rooms with benches. Have a seat and read ahead. When you're ready to tackle the Sistine, stroll through the* **Modern Religious Art** *collection, following signs to the chapel.*

THE SISTINE CHAPEL

The Sistine Chapel contains Michelangelo's ceiling and his huge *Last Judgment*. When Pope Julius II asked Michelangelo to take on this important project, he said, "No, *grazie*." Michelangelo insisted he was a sculptor, not a painter. The Sistine ceiling was a vast undertaking, and he didn't want to do a half-vast job. But the pope pleaded, bribed, and threatened until Michelangelo finally consented, on the condition that he be able to do it all his own way.

Julius had asked for only 12 apostles along the sides of the ceiling, but Michelangelo had a grander vision—the entire history of the world until Jesus. He spent the next four years (1508-1512) craning his neck on scaffolding six stories up, covering the ceiling with frescoes of biblical scenes.

In sheer physical terms, it's an astonishing achievement: 5,900 square feet, with the vast majority done by his own hand. (Raphael only designed most of his rooms, letting assistants do the grunt work.) First, Michelangelo had to design and erect the scaffolding. Any materials had to be hauled up on pulleys. Then, a section of ceiling would be plastered. With fresco—painting on wet plaster—if you don't get it right the first time, you have to scrape the whole thing off and start over. And if you've ever struggled with a ceiling light fixture or worked under a car

The Sistine Schematic

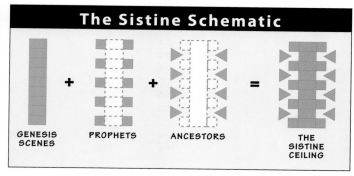

GENESIS SCENES + PROPHETS + ANCESTORS = THE SISTINE CEILING

for even five minutes, you know how heavy your arms get. The physical effort, the paint dripping in his eyes, the creative drain, and the mental stress from a pushy pope combined to almost kill Michelangelo.

But when the ceiling was finished and revealed to the public, it simply blew 'em away. Like the *Laocoön* statue discovered six years earlier, it was unlike anything seen before. It both caps the Renaissance and turns it in a new direction. In perfect Renaissance spirit, it mixes Old Testament prophets with classical figures. But the style is more dramatic, shocking, and emotional than the balanced Renaissance works before it. This is a very personal work—the Gospel according to Michelangelo—but its themes and subject matter are universal. Many art scholars contend that the Sistine ceiling is the single greatest work of art by any one human being.

The Sistine Ceiling:
Understanding What You're Standing Under

The ceiling shows the history of the world before the birth of Jesus. We see God creating the world, creating man and woman, destroying the earth by flood, and so on. God himself, in his purple robe, actually appears in the first five scenes. Along the sides (where the ceiling starts to curve), we see the Old Testament prophets and pagan Greek prophetesses who foretold the coming of Christ. Dividing these scenes and figures are fake niches (a painted 3-D illusion) decorated with nude statue-like figures with symbolic meaning.

The key is to see three simple divisions in the tangle of bodies:

1. The central spine of nine rectangular biblical scenes;

The Sistine Ceiling

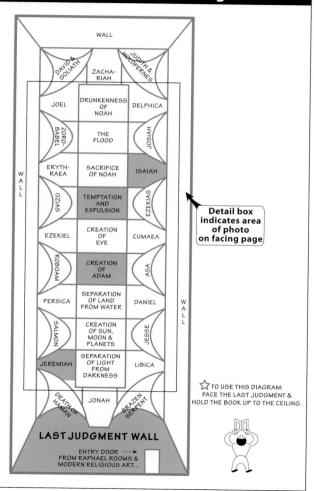

WALL

DAVID & GOLIATH

JUDITH & HOLOFERNES

ZACHA-RIAH

JOEL

DRUNKENNESS OF NOAH

DELPHICA

ZORO-BABEL

THE FLOOD

JOSIAH

W A L L

ERYTH-RAEA

SACRIFICE OF NOAH

ISAIAH

OZIAS

TEMPTATION AND EXPULSION

EZEKIAS

EZEKIEL

CREATION OF EVE

CUMAEA

ROBOAM

CREATION OF ADAM

ASA

PERSICA

SEPARATION OF LAND FROM WATER

DANIEL

W A L L

SALMON

CREATION OF SUN, MOON & PLANETS

JESSE

JEREMIAH

SEPARATION OF LIGHT FROM DARKNESS

LIBICA

DEATH OF HAMAN

JONAH

BRAZEN SERPENT

Detail box indicates area of photo on facing page

☆ TO USE THIS DIAGRAM: FACE THE LAST JUDGMENT & HOLD THE BOOK UP TO THE CEILING.

LAST JUDGMENT WALL

ENTRY DOOR ⟶ FROM RAPHAEL ROOMS & MODERN RELIGIOUS ART...

The Creation of Adam—God and man exchange meaningful eye contact, almost like equals

    2. The line of prophets on either side; and

    3. The triangles between the prophets showing the ancestors of Christ.

▶ *Ready? Ideally, you'll find a place to sit—there are benches along either side. Get oriented by facing the altar with the big* Last Judgment *on the wall—more on that later. Now look up to the ceiling and find the central panel of...*

The Creation of Adam

God and man take center stage in this Renaissance version of creation. Adam, newly formed in the image of God, lounges dreamily in perfect naked innocence. God, with his entourage, swoops in with a swirl of activity (which—with a little imagination—looks like a cross-section of a human brain...quite a strong humanist statement). Their reaching hands are the center of this work. Adam's is limp and passive; God's is strong and forceful, his finger twitching upward with energy. Here is the very moment of creation, as God passes the spark of life to man, the crowning work of his creation.

This is the spirit of the Renaissance. God is not a terrifying giant reaching down to puny and helpless man from way on high. Here they are on an equal plane, divided only by the diagonal bit of sky. God's billowing robe and the patch of green upon which Adam is lying balance each other. They are like two pieces of a jigsaw puzzle, or two long-separated continents, or like the yin and yang symbols finally coming together—uniting, complementing each other, creating wholeness. God and man work together in the divine process of creation.

▶ *This celebration of man permeates the ceiling. Notice the Adonises-come-to-life on the pedestals that divide the central panels.*
    And then came woman.

The Garden of Eden
In one panel, we see two scenes from the Garden of Eden: *Temptation* and *Expulsion*. On the left is the leafy garden of paradise where Adam and Eve lie around blissfully. But the devil comes along—a serpent with a woman's torso—and winds around the forbidden Tree of Knowledge. The temptation to gain new knowledge is too great for these Renaissance people. They eat the forbidden fruit.

At right, a sword-wielding angel drives them from Paradise into the barren plains. They're grieving, but they're far from helpless. Adam's body is thick and sturdy, and we know they'll survive in the cruel world. Adam firmly gestures to the angel, like he's saying, "All right, already! We're going!"

The Nine Scenes from Genesis
Take some time with these central scenes to understand the story that the ceiling tells. They run in sequence, starting at the front:
1. God, in purple, divides the light from darkness.
2. God creates the sun (burning orange) and the moon (pale white, to the right). Oops, I guess there's another moon.
3. God bursts toward us to separate the land and water.
4. God creates Adam.
5. God creates Eve, who dives into existence out of Adam's side.
6. Adam and Eve are tempted, then expelled from the Garden of Eden.
7. Noah kills a ram and stokes the altar fires to make a sacrifice to God.
8. The great flood, sent by God, destroys the wicked, who desperately head for higher ground. In the distance, the ark carries Noah's family to safety. (The blank spot dates to 1793, when a

Prophet Isaiah—stately

Prophet Jeremiah—brooding

nearby gunpowder depot exploded, shaking the building.)

9. Noah's sons see their drunken father. (Perhaps Michelangelo chose to end his work with this scene as a reminder that even the best of men are fallible.)

Prophets

You'll notice that all the figures at the far end of the chapel are a bit smaller than those over *The Last Judgment*. Michelangelo started at the far end, with the Noah scenes. By 1510, he'd finished the first half of the ceiling. When they took the scaffolding down and could finally see what he'd been working on for two years, everyone was awestruck—except Michelangelo. As powerful as his figures are, from the floor they didn't look dramatic enough for Michelangelo. For the other half, he pulled out all the stops.

Compare the Noah scenes (far end), with their many small figures, to the huge images of God at the other end. Similarly, Isaiah (near the lattice screen, marked "Esaias") is stately and balanced, while Jeremiah ("Hieremias," in the corner by *The Last Judgment*) is a dark, brooding figure. This prophet who witnessed the destruction of Israel slumps his chin in his hand and ponders the fate of his people. Like the difference between the stately *Apollo Belvedere* and the excited *Laocoön,* Michelangelo added a new emotional dimension to Renaissance painting.

▶ *The huge fresco on the altar wall (pictured on page 104) is...*

The Last Judgment

In 1535, two decades after he had frescoed the ceiling, Michelangelo was asked to complete his Christian history of the world by painting the final event—the end of time. It's Judgment Day, and Christ—the powerful figure in the center, raising his arm to spank the wicked—has come to find out who's naughty and who's nice. Beneath him, a band of angels blows its trumpets Dizzy Gillespie-style, giving a wake-up call to the sleeping dead. The dead at lower left leave their graves and prepare to be judged. The righteous, on Christ's right hand (the left side of the picture), are carried up to the glories of heaven. The wicked on the other side are hurled down to hell, where demons wait to torture them. Charon, from the underworld of Greek mythology, waits below to ferry the souls of the damned to hell.

It's a grim picture. No one, but no one, is smiling. Even many of the righteous being resurrected (lower left) are either skeletons or cadavers with ghastly skin. The angels have to play tug-of-war with subterranean monsters to drag them from their graves.

Over in hell, the wicked are tortured by gleeful demons. One of the damned (to the right of the trumpeting angels) has an utterly lost expression, as if saying, "Why did I cheat on my wife?!" Two demons grab him around the ankles to pull him down to the bowels of hell, condemned to an eternity of constipation.

But it's the terrifying figure of Christ that dominates this scene. He raises his arm to smite the wicked, sending a ripple of fear through everyone. Even the saints around him—including Mary beneath his arm (whose interceding days are clearly over)—shrink back in terror from this uncharacteristic outburst from loving Jesus. His expression is completely closed, and he turns his head, refusing to even listen to the whining alibis of the damned. Look at Christ's twisting upper body. If this muscular figure looks familiar to you, it's because you've seen it before—the *Belvedere Torso*.

When *The Last Judgment* was unveiled to the public in 1541, it caused a sensation. The pope is said to have dropped to his knees and cried, "Lord, charge me not with my sins when thou shalt come on the Day of Judgment."

And it changed the course of art. The complex composition, with more than 300 figures swirling around the figure of Christ, went far beyond traditional Renaissance balance. And the sheer terror and drama of the scene was a striking contrast to the placid optimism of, say, Raphael's *School of Athens*. Michelangelo had Baroque-en all the rules of the Renaissance, signaling a new era of art.

With the Renaissance fading, the fleshy figures in *The Last Judg-*

ment aroused murmurs of discontent from Church authorities. Michelangelo rebelled by painting his chief critic into the scene—in hell. He's the jackassed demon in the bottom-right corner, wrapped in a snake.

The Last Judgment marks the end of Renaissance optimism epitomized in *The Creation of Adam,* with its innocence and exaltation of man.

Michelangelo himself must have wondered how he would be judged—had he used his God-given talents wisely? Look at St. Bartholomew, the bald, bearded guy at Christ's left foot (our right). In the flayed skin he's holding is a barely recognizable face—the twisted self-portrait of a self-questioning Michelangelo.

The Last Judgment

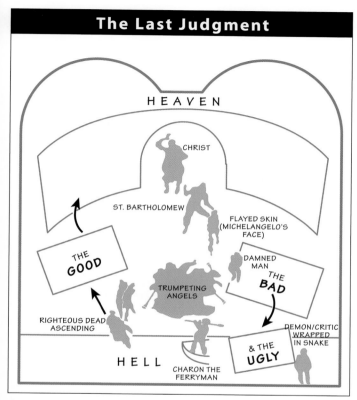

HEAVEN

CHRIST

ST. BARTHOLOMEW

FLAYED SKIN
(MICHELANGELO'S
FACE)

THE
GOOD

DAMNED
MAN
THE
BAD

TRUMPETING
ANGELS

RIGHTEOUS DEAD
ASCENDING

DEMON/CRITIC
WRAPPED
IN SNAKE

& THE
UGLY

HELL

CHARON THE
FERRYMAN

▶ *To return to the museum's main entrance/exit, leave the Sistine through the side door next to the screen (on the left, with your back to the altar). You'll soon find yourself facing the **Long March back to the museum's entrance** (about 15 minutes away). Follow signs to the Pinacoteca, where our tour picks up on the next page.*

PINACOTECA

Like Lou Gehrig batting behind Babe Ruth, the Pinacoteca (Painting Gallery) has to follow the mighty Sistine & Co. But it offers a worthwhile time-lapse walk through the art from medieval to Baroque with just a few stops.

Melozzo da Forlì, *Musician Angels,* 1470s: These playful and delicate frescoes show heavenly musicians in soothing primary colors, even light, and classical purity. Rock on.

Raphael, *The Transfiguration,* 1516-1520: Christ floats above a stumpy mountaintop, visited in a vision by the prophets Moses and Elijah. Peter, James, and John, who wanted visual proof that Jesus was Lord, cower in awe under their savior.

Raphael composes the scene in three descending tiers: Christ, the holiest, is on top, then Peter-James-John, and finally, the nine remaining apostles surround a boy possessed by demons. They direct him and his mother to Jesus for healing.

Raphael died in 1520, and the last thing he painted was the beatific face of Jesus, perhaps the most beautiful Christ in existence. When Raphael was buried, this work accompanied the funeral.

Leonardo da Vinci, *St. Jerome,* c. 1482: Jerome squats in the rocky desert. He's spent too much time alone, fasting and meditating on his sins. His soulful face is echoed by his friend, the roaring lion.

This unfinished work gives us a glimpse of Leonardo's genius. Jerome's emaciated body on the rocks expresses his intense penitence, while his pleading eyes hold a glimmer of hope for divine forgiveness. Leonardo wrote that a good painter must paint two things: "man and the movements of his spirit."

Musician Angels, by Melozzo

St. Jerome, by Leonardo da Vinci

The Transfiguration, by Raphael—perhaps the most beautiful Christ in existence

Caravaggio, *Deposition,* c. 1600-1604: Christ is being buried. In the dark tomb, the faces of his followers emerge, lit by a harsh light. Christ's body has a deathlike color. We see Christ's dirty toes and Nicodemus' wrinkled, sunburned face. A tangle of grief looms in the darkness as Christ's heavy, dead body nearly pulls the whole group with him from the cross into the tomb. After this museum, I know how he feels.

Borghese Gallery Tour

Galleria e Museo Borghese

More than just a great museum, the Borghese Gallery is a beautiful villa set in the greenery of surrounding gardens. You get to see art commissioned by the luxury-loving Borghese family displayed in the very rooms for which it was created.

There's a superb collection of works by Bernini, including his intricately carved *Apollo and Daphne*, a statue that's more air than stone (see facing page). Among the many Caravaggio paintings is the artist's portrait of himself—as a severed head. Frescoes, marble, stucco, and interior design enhance the masterpieces.

This is a place where—regardless of whether you learn a darn thing—you can sit back and enjoy the sheer beauty of the palace and its art.

ORIENTATION

Cost: €17 including booking fees.

Hours: Tue-Sun 9:00-19:00, closed Mon. The museum may be open late one night per week—check online.

Information: +39 06 32810 (for tickets and information), www.galleriaborghese.it.

Reservations Required: Reservations are mandatory. As slots can book up, it's better to reserve sooner rather than later.

It's easiest to book online at www.tosc.it; after booking you'll be emailed a voucher with a bar code that lets you enter at your appointed time. You can also reserve over the telephone (+39 06 32810, press 2 for English).

Getting There: The museum, at Piazzale del Museo Borghese 5, is set in the vast Villa Borghese Gardens (see page 145). A **taxi** drops you along Via Pinciana, 100 yards from the museum. (Tell the cabbie you want "Galleria Borghese," not "Villa Borghese.")

To go by **public transit,** take bus #910 from Termini train station/Piazza della Repubblica to the Puccini stop, walk to the park, turn left, and use the first park entrance.

You can also walk (20 minutes) from the Barberini Metro stop: Walk 10 minutes up Via Veneto, enter the park, and turn right, following signs another 10 minutes to the Borghese Gallery.

Getting In: Arrive early enough to check your bag (it's mandatory—see "Services," below). You can get into the Borghese starting 10 minutes before your appointed time, but you may need to wait in a short line to enter (arriving late could result in forfeiting your reservation). To enter, click the link on your reservation confirmation email to open up the voucher, then scan the bar code on your phone screen at the turnstile. (If you prefer, you can print your voucher at home.)

For crowd control, they may direct you to start either on the ground floor (where this tour begins), or in the Pinacoteca on the upper floor. This tour works equally well in either order.

Tours: Guided English tours may be available (€8; book with your entry reservation). Or consider the museum's excellent 1.5-hour audioguide (€5).

Length of This Tour: This tour takes about an hour; the Borghese rec-

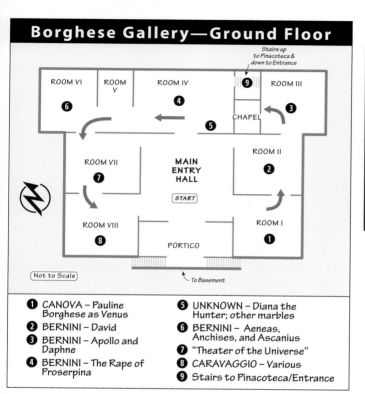

Borghese Gallery—Ground Floor

Stairs up to Pinacoteca & down to Entrance

ROOM VI
ROOM V
ROOM IV
ROOM III

6
4
9

CHAPEL

3

5

ROOM II

ROOM VII
MAIN ENTRY HALL
2

7
START

ROOM I

ROOM VIII
1

8

PORTICO

Not to Scale

To Basement

1 CANOVA – Pauline Borghese as Venus

2 BERNINI – David

3 BERNINI – Apollo and Daphne

4 BERNINI – The Rape of Proserpina

5 UNKNOWN – Diana the Hunter; other marbles

6 BERNINI – Aeneas, Anchises, and Ascanius

7 "Theater of the Universe"

8 CARAVAGGIO – Various

9 Stairs to Pinacoteca/Entrance

ommends a two-hour maximum visit.

Services: Baggage check is free, mandatory, and strictly enforced. Even small purses must be checked.

Cuisine Art: There's a nice café/restaurant under vaulting in the museum basement, near the bag check. A picnic-friendly park with benches is just in front. A few snack stands are in the park, and there's a café at Casa del Cinema a pleasant 10-minute walk downhill from the museum, near the bike-rental stand.

Starring: Sculptures by Bernini and Canova; paintings by Caravaggio, Raphael, and Titian; and the elegant villa itself.

THE TOUR BEGINS

As you visit this palace-in-a-garden, consider its purpose. The pope's nephew, Cardinal Scipione Borghese (1576-1633), wanted to create a place just outside the city where he could showcase his fine art while wining and dining the VIPs of his age. He had the villa built, collected ancient works, and hired the best artists of his day. In pursuing the optimistic spirit of the Renaissance, they invented Baroque.

▶ *Begin the tour on the ground floor, in the main entry hall. (To instead start in the Pinacoteca, find the entrance at the far end of the basement and go directly upstairs to the second floor.)*

Main Entry Hall

The first room that guests saw upon entry was a "theater of the arts"—a multimedia and multi-era extravaganza of art treasures. Baroque frescoes on the ceiling, ancient statues along the walls, and Roman mosaics on the floor capture the essence of the collection.

Five fourth- and fifth-century **mosaics** from a private Roman villa adorn the floor with colorful, festive scenes of slaughter. Gladiators—as famous in their day as the LeBrons and Tom Bradys of our age—fight animals and each other with swords, whips, and tridents. The Greek letter ⊙ marks the dead. Notice some of the gladiators' pro-wrestler nicknames: "Cupid(-o)," "Serpent(-ius)," "Licentious(-us)." On the far left, a scene shows how "Alumnusvic" killed "Mazicinus" and left him lying upside down in a pool of blood.

High up on the wall is a thrilling first-century Greek **sculpture** of a horse falling. The Renaissance-era rider was added by Pietro Bernini, father of the famous Gian Lorenzo Bernini.

▶ *Turn right and head into Room I.*

❶ Antonio Canova, *Pauline Borghese as Venus (Paolina Borghese come Venere)*, 1808

Napoleon's sister went the full monty for the sculptor Canova, scandalizing Europe. ("How could you have done such a thing?!" she was asked. She replied, "The room wasn't cold.") With the famous nose of her conqueror brother, she strikes the pose of Venus as conqueror of men's hearts. Her relaxed afterglow and slight smirk say she's already had her man. The light dent she puts in the mattress makes this goddess human.

Notice the contrasting textures that Canova (1757-1822) gets out of the pure white marble: the rumpled sheet versus her smooth skin, the satiny-smooth pillows and mattress versus the creases in them, her porcelain skin versus the waves of her hair. Canova polished and waxed the marble until it looked as soft and pliable as cloth.

The mythological pose, the Roman couch, the ancient hairdo, and the calm harmony make Pauline the epitome of the Neoclassical style.

▶ *Continue into Room II.*

❷ Gian Lorenzo Bernini, *David,* 1624

Duck! David twists around to put a big rock in his sling. He purses his lips, knits his brow, and winds his body like a spring as his eyes lock onto the target: Goliath, who's somewhere behind us, putting us right in the line of fire.

The face of David is a self-portrait of the 25-year-old Bernini (1598-1680). Looking ready to take on the world, David is charged with the same fighting energy that fueled the missionaries and conquistadors of the Counter-Reformation.

Compared with Michelangelo's *David,* this is unvarnished realism—an unbalanced pose, bulging veins, determined face, and armpit

Canova's cool *Venus* lounges across a rumpled mattress of marble.

Bernini portrays himself as *David,* the giant-slayer ready to take on the world.

hair. Michelangelo's *David* thinks, whereas Bernini's acts—biting his lips, eyes concentrating, and sling stretched. Bernini slays the pretty-boy *David*s of the Renaissance and prepares to invent Baroque.

▶ *Continue into Room III.*

❸ Bernini, *Apollo and Daphne (Apollo e Dafne),* 1625

Apollo—made stupid by Cupid's arrow of love—chases after Daphne, who has been turned off by the "arrow of disgust." Just as he's about to catch her, she calls to her father to save her. Magically, her fingers begin to sprout leaves, her toes become roots, her skin turns to bark, and she transforms into a tree. Frustrated Apollo is in for a rude surprise.

Stand behind the statue to experience it as Bernini originally intended. It's only when you circle around to the front that he reveals the story's surprise ending.

Walk slowly around the statue. Apollo's back leg defies gravity. Bernini chipped away more than half of the block of marble, leaving airy, open spaces. The statue is now in particularly fine form, having spent two years in restoration (described to me as being similar to dental work). It's virtually flawless—yet at the last minute, the sculptor discovered a flaw in the marble that now forms a scar across Daphne's nose.

Bernini carves out some of the chief features of Baroque art. He makes a supernatural event seem realistic. He freezes the scene at its most dramatic, emotional moment. The figures move and twist in unusual poses. He turns the wind machine on, sending Apollo's cape billowing behind him. It's a sculpture group of two, forming a scene, rather than a stand-alone portrait. And the subject is classical. Even in strict Counter-Reformation times, there was always a place for groping, if the subject matter had a moral—this one taught you not to pursue fleeting earthly pleasures. And, besides, Bernini tends to show a lot of skin, but no genitals.

▶ Pass through the cardinal's private chapel and into Room IV.

❹ Bernini, *The Rape of Proserpina* (Il Ratto di Proserpina), 1622

Pluto, king of the Underworld, strides into his realm and shows off his catch—the beautiful daughter of the earth goddess Ceres. His three-headed guard dog, Cerberus (who guards the gates of hell), barks triumphantly. Pluto is squat, thick, and uncouth, with knotted muscles and untrimmed beard. Proserpina pushes her divine molester away and twists to call out for help. His hands dig into her flesh. Tears roll down her cheeks. She wishes she could turn into a tree.

With this work, at the age of 24, Bernini had discovered his Baroque niche. While Renaissance works were designed to be seen from the front, Baroque is theater-in-the-round—full of action, designed to be experienced from every angle as you walk around it. Look how Pluto's fingers dig into Proserpina's frantic body as if it were real flesh. Bernini

Apollo and Daphne—a divine stalker

The Rape of Proserpina—a divine kidnapping

Gian Lorenzo Bernini (1598-1680)

A Renaissance Man in Counter-Reformation times, Bernini almost personally invented the Baroque style, transforming the city of Rome. When visiting Rome, you *will* see Bernini's work.

St. Teresa at S.M. della Vittoria church

Bernini was a child prodigy in his father's sculpting studio, growing up among Europe's rich and powerful. His flamboyant personality endeared him to his cultured employers—the popes in Rome, Louis XIV in France, and Charles I in England. He was extremely prolific, working fast and utilizing an army of assistants.

Despite the fleshiness and sensuality of his works, Bernini was a religious man, seeing his creativity as an extension of God's. In stark contrast to the Protestant world's sobriety, Bernini shamelessly embraced pagan myths and nude goddesses, declaring them all part of the "catholic"—that is, universal—church.

Bernini, a master of multimedia, was a...

- Sculptor (Borghese Gallery and *St. Teresa in Ecstasy,* pictured above and described on page 152)
- Architect (elements of St. Peter's and more)
- Painter (Borghese Gallery)
- Interior decorator (the bronze canopy and more in St. Peter's)
- Civic engineer (he laid out St. Peter's Square, and designed and renovated Rome's fountains in Piazza Navona, Piazza Barberini, Piazza di Spagna, and more).

Even works done by other artists a century later (such as the Trevi Fountain) can be traced indirectly to Bernini, the man who invented Baroque, the "look" of Rome for the next two centuries.

picked out this Carrara marble, knowing that its relative suppleness and ivory hue would lend itself to a fleshy statue.

Other Marbles in Room IV

The statues in the niches are classical originals. ❺ **Diana the Hunter** is a rare Greek original, with every limb and finger intact, from the second century BC. The traditional *contrapposto* pose (weight on one leg) and idealized grace were an inspiration for Neoclassical artists such as Canova, who grew tired of Bernini's Baroque bombast.

Appreciate the beauty of the different types of marble in the room: Bernini's ivory Carrara, purple porphyry emperors and the granite-like columns supporting them, wood-grained pilasters on the walls, and the various colors on the floor—green, red, gray, lavender, and yellow, some grainy, some "marbled" like a steak. Some of the world's most beautiful and durable things have been made from the shells of sea creatures layered in sediment, fossilized into limestone, then baked and crystallized by the pressure of the earth—marble.

▶ *Continue through Room V and into Room VI.*

❻ Bernini, *Aeneas, Anchises, and Ascanius*, 1618-1619

Aeneas' home in Troy is in flames, and he escapes with the three most important things: his family (elderly father Anchises on his shoulder, baby boy Ascanius at his leg), his household gods (the statues in Dad's hands), and the Eternal Flame (carried by his son). They are all in shock, lost in thought, facing an uncertain future. Eventually they'll wind up in Italy, where—according to legend—Aeneas will house the flame in the Temple of Vesta and found the city of Rome.

Bernini was just 20 when he started this, his first major work for Cardinal Borghese. Bernini's portrayal of human flesh—from baby fat to middle-aged muscle to sagging decrepitude—is astonishing. Still, the flat-footed statue just stands there—it lacks the Baroque energy of his more mature work. More lively are the reliefs up at the ceiling, with their dancing, light-footed soldiers with do-si-do shields.

▶ *Enter Room VII.*

❼ "Theater of the Universe"

The room's decor sums up the eclectic nature of the villa. You've got everything here—your Greek statues, your Roman mosaics, even your fake "Egyptian" sphinxes and hieroglyphs (perfectly symmetrical, in good

Neoclassical style). Look out the window past the sculpted gardens at the mesh domes of the aviary, once filled with exotic birds. Cardinal Borghese's vision was to make a place where art, history, music, nature, and science from every place and time would come together in "a theater of the universe."

▶ *Our final stop on the ground floor is Room VIII.*

❽ Caravaggio

This room holds the greatest collection of Caravaggio paintings anywhere. Michelangelo Merisi (1571-1610), nicknamed "Caravaggio" after his hometown, brought Christian saints down to earth with gritty realism.

Circling the room clockwise, trace the course of his brief, dramatic, and sometimes messy life. First, just ahead and on your right as you enter, *Self-Portrait as Bacchus* shows twentysomething Caravaggio as he first arrived in Rome, a poor bohemian enjoying the wild life.

Boy with a Fruit Basket dates from when he eked out a living painting minor figures in other artists' paintings. His specialty? Fruit. Ultrarealistic fruit.

The brash young Caravaggio portrays himself as *Bacchus,* the decadent god of wine.

In 1600, Caravaggio completed his first major commission, a painting of St. Matthew for San Luigi dei Francesi, a church across town (see page 141). Overnight, Caravaggio was famous.

In the next 10 years, Caravaggio pioneered a new age in painting, much as Bernini soon would in sculpture. Caravaggio's unique style combined two striking elements: uncompromising realism and strong light-dark contrasts. His models were ordinary people—*St. John the Baptist* is a nearly nude teenager with dirty feet, whose belly fat wrinkles up as he turns. His depiction of *St. Jerome* is balding and wrinkled. The *Madonna of Palafrenieri* was forbidden to hang in St. Peter's because the boy Jesus was buck naked, and because the Madonna's likeness was inspired by Rome's best-known prostitute. Caravaggio's figures emerge from a dark background, lit by a harsh, unflattering light, which highlights part of the figure, leaving the rest in deep shadows.

Now rich and famous, Caravaggio led a reckless, rock-star existence—trashing hotel rooms and picking fights. In 1606, he killed a man (the details are sketchy) and had to flee Rome. In one of Caravaggio's last paintings, David sticks Goliath's severed head right in our face—and "Goliath" is the artist himself. From exile, Caravaggio appealed to Cardinal Borghese (one of his biggest fans) to get him a pardon. But while returning to Rome, Caravaggio died under mysterious circumstances. Although he lived only to 38, in his short life he'd rocked the world of art.

▶ *Part one of your visit is done. To reach the Pinacoteca, circle around back to Room IV (with Proserpina), find the* ❾ **stairway entry** *in the far-right corner, and spiral up to the...*

Pinacoteca (Painting Gallery)

Several objects in Room XIV give a clearer picture of the man who built the villa (Cardinal Borghese), and the man who helped decorate it (Bernini).

❶ Bernini, Busts of Cardinal Borghese, 1632

Say *grazie* to the man who built this villa, assembled the collection, and hired Bernini to sculpt masterpieces. The cardinal is caught turning as though to greet someone at a party. There's a twinkle in his eye, and he opens his mouth to make a witty comment. This man of the cloth was, in fact, a sophisticated hedonist.

Notice that there are two identical versions of this bust. The first

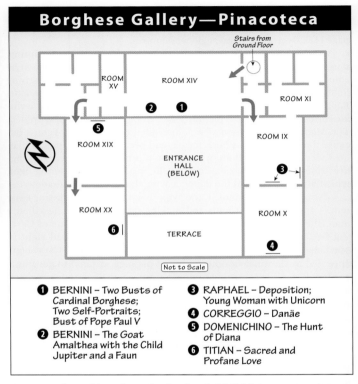

Borghese Gallery—Pinacoteca

❶ BERNINI – Two Busts of Cardinal Borghese; Two Self-Portraits; Bust of Pope Paul V

❷ BERNINI – The Goat Amalthea with the Child Jupiter and a Faun

❸ RAPHAEL – Deposition; Young Woman with Unicorn

❹ CORREGGIO – Danäe

❺ DOMENICHINO – The Hunt of Diana

❻ TITIAN – Sacred and Profane Love

one started cracking along the forehead (visible) just as Bernini was finishing it. *No problema*—Bernini whipped out a replacement in just two weeks.

▶ *Between the busts, find these paintings...*

❶ Bernini, Self-Portraits (*Autoritratto Giovanile* and *Autoritratto in età Matura*) 1623, 1630-1635

Bernini was a master of many media, including painting. The younger Bernini (age 25) looks out a bit hesitantly, as if he's still finding his way in high-class society. (He resembles George Harrison, in more ways than one.) In his next self-portrait (roughly age 35), with a few masterpieces under his belt, Bernini shows himself with more confidence and facial hair—the dashing, vibrant man who would rebuild Rome in Baroque style.

▶ *On the table below, find the smaller...*

❶ Bust of Pope Paul V, 1618

The cardinal's uncle was a more sober man. As pope, Paul V ruled over the artistic era of Caravaggio and Bernini. He reopened an ancient aqueduct, helped steer St. Peter's toward completion, and personally met with Galileo to discuss the heliocentrism controversy.

He was also a patron of the arts with a good eye for talent, who hired Bernini's father. When Paul saw sketches made by little Gian Lorenzo, he announced, "This boy will be the Michelangelo of his age."

▶ *To the right of the Borghese busts, find a small statue of...*

❷ The Goat Amalthea with the Child Jupiter and a Faun
(La Capra Amaltea con Giove Bambino e un Faunetto), 1609/1615

Bernini was barely entering puberty when he made this. (That's about the age when I mastered how to make a Play-Doh snake.) But already its arrangement takes what would become one of Bernini's trademark forms: the sculptural ensemble. The two kids are milking a goat and drinking it. The kids lean one way, the goat the other, with the whole composition contained neatly in a circle of good fun.

▶ *Backtrack to the staircase/elevator and turn right to find Room IX.*

❸ Raphael (Raffaello Sanzio), Deposition
(Deposizione), 1507

Jesus is being taken from the cross. The men struggle heroically to support him while the women support Mary (in purple), who has fainted. Mary Magdalene rushes up to take Christ's hand. The woman who commissioned the painting had recently lost her son. She wanted to show the death of a son and the grief of a mother. We see two different faces of grief—mother Mary faints at the horror, while Mary Magdalene still can't quite believe he's gone.

Enjoy the rich colors—solid reds, greens, blues, and yellows—that set off Christ's porcelain-skin body. In true Renaissance style, Raphael (1483-1520) orders the scene with geometrical perfection. The curve of

Deposition, by Raphael—sacred beauty

Danaë, by Correggio—profane beauty

Jesus' body is echoed by the swirl of Mary Magdalene's hair, and then by the curve of Calvary Hill, where Christ met his fate.

▶ *See Raphael's lighter side in his playful* Portrait of Young Woman with Unicorn, *then continue into Room X.*

❹ Correggio, *Danäe,* c. 1531

Cupid strips Danäe as she spreads her legs to receive a trickle of gold from the smudgy cloud overhead—this was Zeus' idea of intercourse with a human. The sheets are rumpled, and Danäe looks right where the action is with a smile on her face (most unladylike for the time).

▶ *Backtrack through the room with the two cardinal busts, then turn left to find Room XIX. Pause at Domenichino's* ❺ **The Hunt of Diana,** *where half-naked Greek nymphs frolic under the watchful eye of the goddess of the hunt. Then continue frolicking into Room XX to finish with a masterpiece by Titian.*

❻ Titian (Tiziano Vecellio), *Sacred and Profane Love (Amor Sacro e Amor Profano),* c. 1515

While you might guess that the naked woman on the right embodies profane love, that's actually represented by the material girl on the left—with her box of treasures, fortified castle, and dark, claustrophobic landscape. Sacred love is represented by the naked woman who has nothing to hide and enjoys open spaces filled with light, life, a church in the distance, and even a couple of lovers in the field.

The clothed woman at left has recently married, and she cradles a vase filled with jewels representing the riches of earthly love. Her naked twin on the right holds the burning flame of eternal, heavenly love.

Sacred and Profane Love—two women (or are they the same one?) embodying polar opposites

Baby Cupid, between them, playfully stirs the waters.

Symbolically, the steeple on the right points up to the love of heaven, while on the left, soldiers prepare to "storm the castle" of the new bride. Miss Heavenly Love looks jealous.

This exquisite painting expresses the spirit of the Renaissance—that earth and heaven are two sides of the same coin. And here in the Borghese Gallery, that love of earthly beauty can be spiritually uplifting.

Sights

Rome itself is its own best sight. Watching Romans go about their everyday business is endlessly fascinating, whether you ever visit a museum or not.

I've clustered Rome's sights into walkable neighborhoods. Save transit time by grouping your sightseeing according to location. For example, in one great day you can start at the Colosseum, then go to the Forum, then Capitoline Hill, and finally to the Pantheon. Remember that some of Rome's biggest sights (marked with a 📖) are described in detail in the individual walks and tours chapters. A 🎧 means the sight is available as a free audio tour (via my Rick Steves Audio Europe app—see page 11).

State museums in Italy are free to enter once or twice a month, usually on a Sunday, and the Vatican Museums are free on the last Sunday of the month. Free days are actually bad news—they attract crowds. Check state museum websites in advance and make a point to avoid their free days.

ANCIENT ROME

The core of ancient Rome, where the grandest monuments were built, is between the Colosseum and Capitoline Hill. In Caesar's day, this was "downtown Rome—citizens shopped at the bustling malls of the Forum, razzed gladiators at the Colosseum, and climbed Capitoline Hill to sacrifice a goat to Jupiter.

Today, this area is home to acres and acres of the planet's most famous ruins and sights. I've listed them from south to north, starting with the biggies—the Colosseum and Forum—and continuing up to Capitoline Hill and Piazza Venezia. Between the Capitoline and the river is the former Jewish Ghetto. Metro stop Colosseo and local buses put you right in the thick of the action.

Ancient Core

▲▲▲Colosseum (Colosseo)

This 2,000-year-old building is the classic example of Roman engineering. Used as a venue for entertaining the masses, this colossal, functional stadium is one of Europe's most recognizable landmarks.

    📖 See the Colosseum Tour chapter or 🎧 download my free audio tour.

▲Arch of Constantine

This well-preserved arch, which stands between the Colosseum and the Forum, commemorates a military coup and, more important, the acceptance of Christianity by the Roman Empire. When the ambitious Emperor Constantine (who had a vision that he'd win under the sign of the cross) defeated his rival Maxentius in AD 312, Constantine became sole emperor of the Roman Empire and legalized Christianity. The arch is free to see—always open and viewable.

▲▲▲Roman Forum (Foro Romano)

This is ancient Rome's birthplace and civic center, and the common ground between Rome's famous seven hills. Just about anything important that happened in ancient Rome happened here.

    📖 See the Roman Forum Tour chapter or 🎧 download my free audio tour.

Rome Sightseeing Tips

Rome is doing its best to cope with an ever-increasing number of visitors, but especially in peak season you'll encounter lines, crowds, and exasperating changes to ticketing and tour procedures. These tips will help you use your time and money efficiently.

Skip the Colosseum: While it sounds like a sacrilege, a visit to the interior of the Colosseum may not be worth suffering through the mob scene. Half the thrill of the Colosseum is seeing it from outside (free and easy at any time).

Advance Tickets and Reservations: Some sights require advance booking while at others it's necessary to avoid long lines. At a few key sights, reservations are either required or highly recommended: the Colosseum, Borghese Gallery, Vatican Museums (with the Sistine Chapel), and on weekends, the Pantheon (for specifics, see the individual tour chapters or listings).

Forum/Palatine Hill: These two sights share an admission ticket. Unless you buy a Full Experience ticket (see page 26), you must see them together on a single visit (don't exit the Forum and try to reenter at Palatine Hill).

Roma Pass: I'd skip this pass, which you'll see advertised.

Sights with Fewer Crowds: Can't get reservations (or just can't stand crowds)? Rome has many magnificent attractions without the hordes. Try the Baths of Caracalla, National Museum of Rome, Trajan's Market, or Ostia Antica. Even in peak season, you'll often be all alone with the wonders of the ancient world, wondering, "Where is everyone?"

Check Sight Hours: Rome's sights have notoriously variable hours. It's smart to check each sight's website in advance. On holidays, expect shorter hours or closures.

Churches: Many churches, which have divine art and free entry, open early (around 7:00-7:30), close for lunch (roughly 12:00-15:30), and close late (about 19:00). Kamikaze tourists maximize their sightseeing hours by visiting churches before 9:00 or late in the day; during the siesta, they see major sights that stay open all day. Dress modestly.

Picnic Discreetly: Public drinking and eating are not allowed at major sights. To avoid a fine, choose an empty piazza or a park for your picnic.

Ancient Rome

▲Palatine Hill (Monte Palatino)

The hill overlooking the Forum was the home of the emperors and now contains a museum, scant (but impressive when understood) remains of imperial palaces, and a view of the Circus Maximus.

We get our word "palace" from this hill where the emperors lived in a sprawling 150,000-square-foot palace. You'll wander among vague outlines of rooms, courtyards, fountains, a banquet hall with a heated floor, and a sunken stadium. The throne room was the center of power for an empire of 50 million that stretched from England to Africa. The Palatine Museum's statues and frescoes help you imagine the former luxury of this now-desolate hilltop. In one direction are expansive views over the dusty Circus Maximus chariot course. In the other are photogenic views of the Forum.

Supposedly, Romulus and Remus were suckled by a she-wolf on Palatine Hill, raised by shepherds, and grew to found the city in 753 BC. Quaint legend? Well, here on Palatine Hill, you can see the remains of shepherds' huts, dated around 850 BC. The legend enters into history.

▶ *€18 combo-ticket also includes the Forum and Colosseum (must buy in advance, valid 24 hours). A €24 Full Experience ticket adds some smaller sights (which may have shorter hours and random closed days) and is valid for two days. Daily from 9:00 until one hour before sunset: April-Aug until 19:15, Sept until 19:00, Oct until 18:30, Nov-Feb until 16:30, March until 17:30; last entry one hour before closing. The main entrance is 150 yards south of the Colosseum on Via di San Gregorio. You can also enter the Palatine from within the Roman Forum, near the Arch of Titus. Metro: Colosseo, +39 06 3996 7700, information: www.parcocolosseo.it, tickets: www.coopculture.it.*

Bocca della Verità

The legendary "Mouth of Truth" at the Church of Santa Maria in Cosmedin—a few blocks southwest of the other sights listed here—can be crowded with mindless "selfie-stick" travelers. Stick your hand in the mouth of the gaping stone face in the porch wall. As the legend goes (and was popularized by the 1953 film *Roman Holiday*), if you're a liar, your hand will be gobbled up.

▶ *€0.50 suggested donation, always viewable through church gate, accessible daily 9:30-17:50, Piazza Bocca della Verità 18, near the north end of Circus Maximus.*

Capitoline Hill and Piazza Venezia

The geographical (if not spiritual) center of Rome, this area straddles the ancient and modern worlds. Capitoline Hill was ancient Rome's political center, and today is home to several distinguished sights. At the foot of the hill is modern Piazza Venezia, a vast, traffic-filled square where four major boulevards meet. Between the hill and the piazza squats the massive white Victor Emmanuel Monument, 20 stories tall.

Capitoline Hill & Piazza Venezia

Villa Colonna

S. APOSTOLI

To Piazza del Popolo

VIA DEL CORSO

GALLERIA DORIA PAMPHILJ

V. BATTISTI

VIA 4 NOVEMBRE

VIA 4 NOVEMBRE

#64, 40 (B)

Piazza Venezia

VIA PLEBISCITO

Largo Magnanapoli

ROMAN HOUSE

SS NOME DI MARIA

PALAZZO VENEZIA

← MUSSOLINI'S BALCONY

VIA NAZIONALE

(B) #64, 85

S. MARIA DI LORETO

(T)

To Gesù & Pantheon

SAN MARCO

TRAJAN'S COLUMN

MUSEUM OF IMPERIAL FORUMS & TRAJAN'S MARKET

(T) #8

(B) #64

ENTRANCE →

VICTOR EMMANUEL MONUMENT

TRAJAN'S

FORUM

VIA ALESSANDRINA

VIA D'ARACOELI

ROME FROM THE SKY ELEVATOR ■

STA. MARIA ARACOELI

#85, 87, 118 &186

(B)

CAESAR'S FORUM

VIA DEI FORI IMPERIALI

MICHELANGELOS GRAND STAIRCASE

STATUE

PALAZZO NUOVO

DRINKING FOUNTAIN

Piazza del Campidoglio

To Teatro di Marcello

Piazza Caffarelli

MAMERTINE PRISON

To Colosseum & (M)

PUBLIC CAFÉ ENTRANCE

VIA TEATRO MARCELLO

PALAZZO SENATORIO

SANTI LUCA E MARTINA

CAPITOLINE MUSEUMS PALAZZO DEI CONSERVATORI

TABULARIUM

SEASONAL ENTRY

CAFÉ

ARCH OF SEPTIMIUS SEVERUS

ROMAN FORUM

FORO ROMANO

FORUM EXIT

100 Meters

100 Yards

Piazza d. Consolazione

Capitoline Hill

Of Rome's famous seven hills, this is the smallest, tallest, and most famous—home of the ancient Temple of Jupiter and the center of city government for 2,500 years. There are several ways to get to the top of Capitoline Hill. If you're coming from the north (from Piazza Venezia), take Michelangelo's impressive stairway to the right of the big, white Victor Emmanuel Monument. Coming from the southeast (the Roman Forum), take the steep staircase near the Arch of Septimius Severus. From near Trajan's Forum along Via dei Fori Imperiali, take the winding road. All three converge at the top, in the square called ▲ **Piazza del Campidoglio** (kahm-pee-DOHL-yoh).

This square, once the religious and political center of ancient Rome, is still the home of the city's government and resonates with history. In the 1530s, the pope called on Michelangelo to reestablish this square as a grand center. Michelangelo placed the ancient equestrian statue of Marcus Aurelius as its focal point—very effective. (The original statue is now in the adjacent museum.) Notice how the twin buildings on either side (now the Capitoline Museums) angle inward, drawing the visitor into this welcoming space. Behind the replica of the statue is the mayoral palace (Palazzo Senatorio).

The hill-topping **Santa Maria in Aracoeli** church houses a much-loved wooden statue (actually a copy) of the Baby Jesus (*Santo Bambino*) that locals venerate at Christmastime. The daunting 125-step staircase up to the church's front door was once climbed—on their knees—by Roman women who wished for a child. Today, they don't...and Italy has Europe's lowest birthrate.

▶ *The Campidoglio is always open and free. Santa Maria in Aracoeli church is free, daily 9:00-18:30, 9:30-17:30 in winter, +39 06 6976 3839.*

▲▲▲Capitoline Museums (Musei Capitolini)

Some of ancient Rome's most famous statues and art are housed in the two palaces that flank the equestrian statue in the Campidoglio.

In the Conservatori wing, you'll see the original statue of the she-wolf suckling the twins Romulus and Remus. This is the oldest known statue of this symbol of ancient Rome. Also in the museum is the original statue of Marcus Aurelius (the one in the Campidoglio is a copy), the greatest surviving equestrian statue of antiquity. Marcus was both an emperor (ruled AD 161-180) and a philosopher.

Piazza del Campidoglio atop Capitoline Hill   A sliver of the vast Capitoline Museums

A bust of Emperor Commodus as Hercules depicts Marcus's bratty son. Commodus (ruled AD 180-192) earned a reputation for cruelty, dressing up like a demi-god and beating innocent people to death with his Hercules club. The well-known *Boy Extracting a Thorn* depicts one of those mundane moments in life when we'd give anything for tweezers.

In the Nuovo wing, the *Dying Gaul* (a first-century BC copy of a Greek original) shows a warrior wounded in battle. He holds himself upright, but barely, watching helplessly as his life ebbs away.

The museum also displays the scant remains of Capitoline Hill's once-massive, renowned Temple of Jupiter. Don't miss the Tabularium, the ancient Roman archive, which offers a superb view of the Forum.

▶ *€15, daily 9:30-19:30, last entry one hour before closing, videoguide-€7, +39 06 0608, www.museicapitolini.org.*

▲Mamertine Prison (Carcer Tullianum Museum)

This 2,500-year-old cistern-like prison on Capitoline Hill is where, according to Christian tradition, the Romans imprisoned Saints Peter and Paul. Today it's a small but impressive archaeological site using the latest technology to illustrate what you might unearth when digging in Rome: a pagan sacred site, an ancient Roman prison, an early Christian pilgrimage destination, or a medieval church. This pricey sight is a good value for pilgrims and antiquities wonks.

▶ *€10, includes videoguide, €24 combo-ticket includes Colosseum and Roman Forum/Palatine Hill, daily 9:00-17:00, may stay open later in summer, Clivo Argentario 1, +39 06 698 961.*

Piazza Venezia

This vast square, dominated by the big, white Victor Emmanuel Monument, is a major transportation hub and the focal point of modern Rome. With your back to the monument (you'll get the best views from the terrace by the guards and eternal flame), look down Via del Corso, the city's axis, surrounded by Rome's classiest shopping district.

In the 1930s, Benito Mussolini whipped up Italy's nationalistic fervor from a **balcony** above the square (it's the less-grand building on the left). Fascist masses filled the square screaming, "Four more years!"—or something like that.

▲Victor Emmanuel Monument

This oversized monument to Italy's first king, built to celebrate the 50th anniversary of the country's unification in 1861, was part of Italy's push to overcome the new country's strong regionalism and create a national identity. The scale of the monument is over the top: 200 feet high, 500 feet wide. The 43-foot-long statue of the king on his high horse is one of the biggest equestrian statues in the world. The king's moustache forms an arc five feet long, and a person could sit within the horse's hoof. At the base of this statue, Italy's Tomb of the Unknown Soldier (flanked by

Locals love to hate the grandiose Victor Emmanuel Monument, but the view from the top is fantastic.

Italian flags and armed guards) is watched over by the goddess Roma (with the gold mosaic background).

The classic experience is to climb the front stairs for views. For the grandest 360-degree view—even better than from the top of St. Peter's dome—pay to ride the **Rome from the Sky** (Roma dal Cielo) elevator. The elevator ticket includes entry to the **Museum of the Risorgimento,** which fills two giant circular rooms and a long hallway deep inside the monument. Statues, paintings, posters, tattered flags, and other artifacts help tell the story of how Italy was united, starting in the 19th century.

▶ *Free to climb stairs of monument, €12 to ride elevator and enter museum (access to museum limited to small groups entering twice hourly, www.risorgimento.it). Open daily 9:30-19:30, last elevator ticket sold 45 minutes before closing, a few WCs scattered throughout, +39 06 0608, https://vive.beniculturali.it.*

Jewish Quarter

From the 16th through the 19th century, Rome's Jewish population was forced to live in a cramped ghetto at an often-flooded bend of the Tiber River. While the medieval Jewish ghetto is long gone, this area—between Capitoline Hill and the Campo de' Fiori—is still home to Rome's synagogue and fragments of its Jewish heritage.

The **synagogue** stands proudly on the spot where the medieval Jewish community was sequestered for more than 300 years. The site of a historic visit by Pope John Paul II, this synagogue features a fine interior and a museum filled with artifacts of Rome's Jewish community. The only way to visit the synagogue—unless you're here for daily prayer service—is with a tour.

Great Synagogue—modern Judaism

Rome from the Sky elevator for 360° views

▶ €11 includes museum audioguide and guided tour of synagogue; Sun-Thu 10:00-18:00, Fri until 16:00; shorter hours Oct-March, closed Sat year-round and on Jewish holidays; last entry 45 minutes before closing, English tours usually at :15 past the hour, 30 minutes, confirm at ticket counter, modest dress required, on Lungotevere dei Cenci, +39 06 6840 0661, www.museoebraico.roma.it. Walking tours of the ghetto are also offered—check schedule online. ◖ Or, download my free Jewish Ghetto Walk audio tour.

The Imperial Forums and Nearby

Though the original Roman Forum is the main attraction for today's tourists, there are several more ancient forums nearby, known collectively as "The Imperial Forums." As Rome grew from a village to an empire, it outgrew the Roman Forum. Several energetic emperors built their own forums complete with temples, shopping malls, government buildings, statues, monuments, and piazzas.

Today the ruins are out in the open, never crowded, and free to look down on from street level at any time, any day. The forums stretch in a line along Via dei Fori Imperiali, from Piazza Venezia to the Colosseum. The once-noisy boulevard is a pleasant walk, since it is closed to private vehicles—and, on Sundays, to all traffic. If you'll be here in the evening, consider taking in a sound-and-light show (see page 173).

▲▲Trajan's Column, Market, and Museum of the Imperial Forums

Trajan's 140-foot column—the grandest from antiquity—was the centerpiece of a complex of buildings built by the Emperor Trajan (who ruled AD 98-117). After Trajan conquered and looted central Europe, he returned to Rome with his booty and shook it all over the city. He built a forum of markets, civic buildings, and temples to rival the nearby Roman Forum.

Trajan's Column is carved with a spiral relief trumpeting Trajan's exploits. It winds upward—more than 200 yards long with 2,500 figures—from the assembling of the army to the victory sacrifice at the top. A gleaming bronze statue of Trajan once capped the column, where St. Peter stands today.

The rest of Trajan's Forum is now ruined and a bit underwhelming, except for one grand structure—**Trajan's Market,** a semicircular brick building nestled into the cutaway curve of Quirinal Hill. Part shopping mall, part warehouse, part office building, this was where

Trajan's Column and Forum

Michelangelo's *Moses* at St. Peter-in-Chains

Romans could browse through goods from every corner of their vast empire—exotic fruits from Africa, spices from Asia, and fish-and-chips from Londinium. The 13 arches of the lower level may have held produce; the 26 windows above lit a covered arcade; and the roofline housed more stalls—150 shops in all.

The nearby **Museum of the Imperial Forums** houses discoveries from the forums built by the different emperors. Its well-displayed exhibits help put all these ruins in context. It also allows you to walk outside, atop, and amid the ruins, making this a rare opportunity to get up close to Trajan's Market and Forum.

▶ *Trajan's Column, Forum, and Market (always free and viewable) are just a few steps off Piazza Venezia, near the Victor Emmanuel Monument. The Museum of the Imperial Forums is at Via IV Novembre 94, up the staircase from Trajan's Column (€15, daily 9:30-19:30, last entry one hour before closing, +39 06 0608, www.mercatiditraiano.it).*

▲The Roman House at Palazzo Valentini
(Le Domus Romane di Palazzo Valentini)

For a quality (air-conditioned) experience, duck into this underground series of ancient spaces at the base of Trajan's Column. The 50-minute tour with good English narration and evocative lighting features scant remains of an elegant ancient Roman house and bath. The highlight is a small theater where you'll learn the entire story depicted by the 2,600 figures that parade around the 650-foot relief carved onto Trajan's Column.

▶ *€12; Wed-Mon 10:00-19:00, closed Tue, last entry one hour before closing, may have shorter hours off-season; departures hourly but not* *all in English—check online, limited group sizes—reservations smart (€1.50 fee), +39 06 2276 1280, www.palazzovalentini.it.*

▲Monti Neighborhood

Tucked behind the Imperial Forums (between Trajan's Column and the Cavour Metro stop) is a quintessentially Roman district called Monti. During the day, check out Monti's array of funky shops and grab a quick lunch. In the evening, linger over a fine meal (see page 187 for recommendations). Later at night, the streets froth with happy young drinkers.

▲▲St. Peter-in-Chains Church (San Pietro in Vincoli)

A church was first built on this spot in the fifth century, to house the chains that once restrained St. Peter. Today's church, restored in the 15th century, is famous for its Michelangelo statue of Moses, intended for the (unfinished) tomb of Pope Julius II. Check out the chains under the high altar, then focus on mighty Moses.

In 1505, the egomaniacal Pope Julius II asked Michelangelo to build a massive tomb—a free-standing pyramid, with 40 statues, to stand in the center of St. Peter's Basilica. Michelangelo labored on it for four decades, but got distracted by other gigs such as the Sistine Chapel. In 1542, Michelangelo and his assistants half-heartedly pieced together a few remnants in St. Peter-in-Chains.

What we see today is not a full-blown 3-D pyramid but a 2-D wall monument framing a handful of statues. A statue of Pope Julius reclines on his fake coffin midway up the wall and looks down at the monument's highlight—*Moses*. Just returned from meeting face-to-face with God, Moses senses trouble. Slowly he turns to see his followers worshipping a golden calf. As his anger builds, he glares and cradles the Ten Commandments, about to spring out of his chair and spank the naughty Children of Israel.

Why does Moses have horns? Centuries ago, the Hebrew word for "rays" was mistranslated as "horns." But it also captures an air of *terribilità*, a kind of scary charisma possessed by Moses, Pope Julius...and Michelangelo.

▶ *Free, daily 7:15-12:30 & 15:00-19:00, Oct-March until 18:00, modest dress required; the church is a 10-minute uphill walk from the Colosseum, or a shorter, simpler walk (but with more steps) from the Cavour Metro stop; +39 06 9784 4950.*

PANTHEON NEIGHBORHOOD

In the area around the Pantheon you see all the city's historic layers on display—ancient ruins, medieval lanes, Baroque fountains, and modern Romans at work and play. This neighborhood stretches from the Tiber River through Campo de' Fiori and Piazza Navona, past the Pantheon to the Trevi Fountain. To get here by taxi or bus (#64 or #40), aim for the large square called Largo Argentina, a few blocks south of the Pantheon.

Besides being home to ancient sites and historic churches, the area around the Pantheon is another part of Rome with an urban village feel. Wander narrow streets, sample the many shops and eateries, and gather with the locals in squares marked by bubbling fountains. It's especially enjoyable in the evening, with a gelato in hand, when restaurants bustle and streets are jammed with foot traffic.

For a good introductory walk through the neighborhood, □ see my Heart of Rome Walk on page 15 and ∩ download my free Heart of Rome Walk audio tour.

▲▲▲ Pantheon

For the greatest look at the splendor of Rome, antiquity's best-preserved interior is a must. Built two millennia ago, this influential domed temple served as the model for Michelangelo's dome of St. Peter's and many others.

Exterior: The Pantheon was a Roman temple dedicated to all (*pan*) of the gods (*theos*), a one-stop-shopping temple where you could worship any of the gods whose statues decorated the niches. The original temple was built in 27 BC by Emperor Augustus' son-in-law, Marcus Agrippa (as the Latin inscription above the columns proclaims). The structure we see

The Pantheon—Rome's best-preserved temple   The open-air oculus in the Pantheon's dome

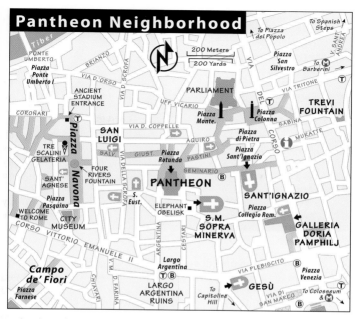

today dates from around AD 120, built by Emperor Hadrian. The 40-foot-high columns were taken from an Egyptian temple.

Interior—The Dome: The awe-inspiring dome is mathematically perfect: 142 feet tall and 142 feet wide. It rests atop a circular base; imagine a basketball set inside a wastebasket so that it just touches bottom. The dome is constructed from concrete, a Roman invention. The base is 23 feet thick and made from heavy travertine concrete, while the top is five feet thick and made from light volcanic pumice. The square indentations (or coffers) reduce the weight of the dome without compromising strength. At the top, the oculus, or eye-in-the-sky, is the building's only light source and is almost 30 feet across. The Pantheon also contains the world's greatest Roman column—the pillar of light from the oculus.

This dome is perhaps the most influential in art history. It inspired Brunelleschi's Florence cathedral dome, Michelangelo's dome of St. Peter's, and even the capitol dome of Washington, DC.

The Pantheon dome rises from thick walls at the base, to thin at the top, to the open-air oculus.

The Rest: The marble floor—with its design of alternating circles and squares—is largely original. It has holes in it and slants toward the edges to let the rainwater drain.

Early in the Middle Ages, the Pantheon became a Christian church (from "all the gods" to "all the martyrs"), which means it's been in continual use for nearly 1,900 years. To the right of the altar is the tomb of Italy's first modern king, Victor Emmanuel II (*"Padre della Patria,"* father of the fatherland), and to the left is Umberto I (son of the father). Also to the left of the altar, the artist Raphael lies buried, in a lighted glass niche.

▶ *€5, free first Sun of the month; daily 9:00-19:00, closed for Mass Sat at 17:00 and Sun at 10:30; tickets sold on-site or online at https:// portale.museiitaliani.it; for guided tours and audioguides, see www. pantheonroma.com.* ⌒ *Or, download my free audio tour.*

▲▲Churches near the Pantheon
Several interesting churches cluster near the Pantheon, with art by Michelangelo and Caravaggio, and connections with St. Ignatius and the Jesuit order. Modest dress is recommended.

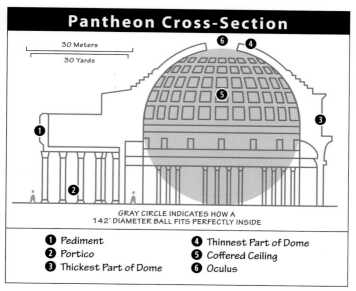

Pantheon Cross-Section

30 Meters

30 Yards

GRAY CIRCLE INDICATES HOW A
142' DIAMETER BALL FITS PERFECTLY INSIDE

1 Pediment
2 Portico
3 Thickest Part of Dome
4 Thinnest Part of Dome
5 Coffered Ceiling
6 Oculus

The **Church of San Luigi dei Francesi** has a magnificent chapel painted by Caravaggio. In *The Calling of St. Matthew* (left wall), Jesus walks into a dingy bar, raises his arm, and points to a sheepish Matthew, calling him to discipleship. The other two paintings show where Matthew's call led him—writing a Gospel of Jesus' life, and eventually giving up his own life for the Christian cause (free, Mon-Sat 9:30-12:45 & 14:30-18:30, Sun from 11:30, between Pantheon and north end of Piazza Navona, www.saintlouis-rome.net). The only Gothic church in Rome is the **Church of Santa Maria sopra Minerva,** with a little-known Michelangelo statue, *Christ Bearing the Cross* (free, daily 9:00-12:00 & 16:00-19:00; on a little square behind the Pantheon, to the east, www.santamariasopraminerva.it). The **Church of Sant'Ignazio,** several blocks east of the Pantheon, is a riot of Baroque illusions with a false dome (free, daily 9:00-19:00, www.chiesasantignazio.it). A few blocks away, across Corso Vittorio Emanuele, is the rich and Baroque **Gesù Church,** headquarters of the Jesuits in Rome (free, generally Mon-Sat 7:30-12:30 & 17:00-19:30, Sun 9:00-12:30 & 17:00-20:00, interesting daily ceremony at 17:30 at the Tomb of St. Ignatius, www.chiesadelgesu.org).

▲Galleria Doria Pamphilj

This underappreciated art-filled palace lies in the heart of the old city and boasts absolutely no tourist crowds. Through an audioguide, the prince lovingly narrates his family's story as you tour the palace and its world-class art.

Don't miss Velázquez's intense, majestic, ultrarealistic portrait of the family founder, Innocent X. It stands alongside an equally impressive bust of the pope by the father of the Baroque art style, Gian Lorenzo Bernini. Stroll through a mini-Versailles-like hall of mirrors to more paintings. In one impressive room you'll see works by Titian, Raphael, and Caravaggio.

▶ *€14, includes worthwhile 1.5-hour audioguide, daily 9:00-19:00, last entry one hour before closing, closed third Wed of month, elegant café, between Sant'Ignazio Church and Piazza Venezia—from Piazza Venezia walk 2 blocks up Via del Corso to #305, +39 06 679 7323, www. dopart.it/roma.*

Piazzas and Fountains

These are all covered in more detail in 📖 the Heart of Rome Walk chapter and 🎧 my free audio tour.

▲▲**Campo de' Fiori:** One of Rome's most colorful spots, this bohemian piazza hosts a fruit-and-vegetable market in the morning, cafés in the evening, and pub crawlers at night.

▲▲**Piazza Navona:** This long, oval-shaped piazza—dotted with fountains and surrounded by open-air restaurants—attracts both locals and tourists, especially in the evening.

▲**Trevi Fountain:** The bubbly Baroque fountain, worth ▲▲ by night, is a minor sight to art scholars...but a major nighttime gathering spot for teens on the make and tourists tossing coins.

VATICAN CITY AND NEARBY

Vatican City contains the Vatican Museums (with Michelangelo's Sistine Chapel) and St. Peter's Basilica (with Michelangelo's exquisite *Pietà*). It sits on the west bank of the Tiber in an otherwise nondescript neighborhood. Nearby are a few lesser sights. The Ottaviano Metro stop

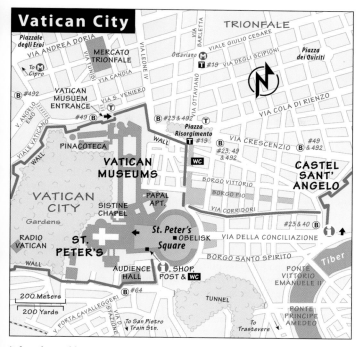

is handy, and buses #40, #64, #49, #23, and #492 stop in the area.

Modest dress is technically required of men, women, and children throughout Vatican City, even outdoors. The policy is strictly enforced in the Sistine Chapel and at St. Peter's Basilica.

▲▲▲St. Peter's Basilica (Basilica San Pietro)

There is no doubt: This is the richest and grandest church on earth. To call it vast is like calling Einstein smart.

📖 See the St. Peter's Basilica Tour chapter or 🎧 download my free audio tour.

▲▲▲Vatican Museums (Musei Vaticani)

The four miles of displays in this immense museum complex—from an-

St. Peter's at night is magic.

Castel Sant'Angelo—a former tomb

cient statues to Christian frescoes to modern paintings—culminate in the Raphael Rooms and Michelangelo's glorious Sistine Chapel.

📖 See the Vatican Museums Tour chapter or 🎧 download my Sistine Chapel and Vatican Museums audio tours.

▲Castel Sant'Angelo

Built as a tomb for the emperor Hadrian, used through the Middle Ages as a castle, prison, and place of last refuge for popes under attack, and today a museum, this giant pile of ancient bricks is packed with history. The structure itself is striking, the opulent papal rooms are dramatic (and cool inside during the summer), and the views up top are some of the best in Rome.

A one-way route circulates visitors through the medieval and then the ancient parts of the monument. After climbing some ramparts, you then pass the little 19th-century military museum. Next, enter medieval rooms built for the pope. The papal library was painted by followers of Raphael. Its fine ceiling features grotesque-style figures made trendy in the 16th century after the discovery of Nero's Golden House (his palace near the Colosseum). Next is the pope's treasury; imagine the huge armored box containing the loot of the medieval age. Eventually you reach the rooftop terrace with the statue of the Archangel Michael sheathing his sword—and one of the top views anywhere of Rome and St. Peter's Basilica.

▶ *€12, more with special exhibits, Tue-Sun 9:00-19:30, closed Mon, last entry one hour before closing, near Vatican City, 10-minute walk from St. Peter's Square at Lungotevere Castello 50, Metro: Lepanto or bus #40 or #64, café, +39 06 681 9111, www.castelsantangelo.beniculturali.it.*

The Villa Borghese Gardens form the northern border of tourists' Rome. Several sights lie inside the landscaped park, while others ring its southern perimeter, clustered around the Spanish Steps, Via Veneto, and Piazza del Popolo. The area has some of Rome's classiest fashion boutiques. Metro stops Spagna, Barberini, and Flaminio serve the neighborhood.

▲Villa Borghese Gardens

Rome's somewhat scruffy three-square-mile "Central Park" is great for its quiet shaded paths and for people-watching plenty of modern-day Romeos and Juliets. The best entrance is at the head of Via Veneto (Metro: Barberini, then 10-minute walk up Via Veneto and through the old Roman wall at Porta Pinciana, or catch a cab to Via Veneto—Porta Pinciana). There you'll find a cluster of buildings with a café, a kiddie arcade, and bike rental (€4/hour). Rent a bike or, for romantics, a pedaled rickshaw (*risciò*, €12/hour). Some sights require paid admission, including the Borghese Gallery, Rome's zoo, the National Gallery of Modern Art, and the Etruscan Museum.

▲▲▲Borghese Gallery (Galleria Borghese)

This plush museum, filling a cardinal's mansion in the park, offers one of Europe's most sumptuous art experiences. You'll enjoy a collection of world-class Baroque sculpture, including Bernini's *David* and his excited statue of Apollo chasing Daphne, as well as paintings by Caravaggio, Raphael, Titian, and Rubens. The museum's mandatory reservation system keeps crowds to a manageable size.

📖 For more on reservations, as well as a self-guided tour, see the Borghese Gallery Tour chapter.

Capuchin Crypt (Cripta dei Frati Cappuccini)

If you want to see artistically arranged bones in Italy, this (while overpriced) is the place. The crypt is below the Church of Santa Maria della Immacolata Concezione on the tree-lined Via Veneto, just up from Piazza Barberini. The bones of about 4,000 friars who died in the 1700s are in the basement, all lined up in a series of six crypts for the delight—or disgust—of the always-wide-eyed visitor.

Before the crypt, a six-room museum covers the history of the Capuchins, a branch of the Franciscan order. For most travelers, how-

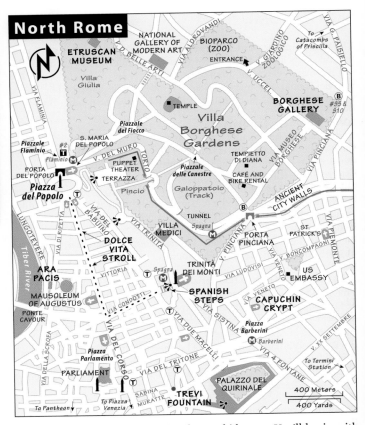

North Rome

ETRUSCAN MUSEUM

NATIONAL GALLERY OF MODERN ART

BIOPARCO (ZOO)
ENTRANCE

To Catacombs of Priscilla

VIA ALDROVANDI

VIA G. PAISIELLO

VIA DELLE BELLE ARTI

V. GIARDINO ZOOLOGICO

V. UCCEL

Villa Giulia

TEMPLE

Villa Borghese Gardens

BORGHESE GALLERY
#95 & 910

VIA FLAMINIA

Piazzale del Fiocco

S. MARIA DEL POPOLO

Piazzale Flaminio
#2

Flaminio

V. DEL MURO

PUPPET THEATER

TERRAZZA

TORTO

Piazzale delle Canestre

TEMPIETTO DI DIANA

CAFÉ AND BIKE RENTAL

VIA MUSEO BORGHESE

VIA PINCIANA

PORTA DEL POPOLO

Piazza del Popolo

Pincio

Galoppatoio (Track)

ANCIENT CITY WALLS

VIA DE' BABUINO

VIA DI RIPETTA

VIA TRINITA

VILLA MEDICI

Spagna

TUNNEL

PORTA PINCIANA

ST. PATRICK'S

VIA PIEMONTE

LUNGOTEVERE

Tiber River

DOLCE VITA STROLL

VITTORIA

Spagna

TRINITÀ DEI MONTI

V. BONCOMPAGNI

US EMBASSY

VIA LUDOVISI

ARA PACIS

MAUSOLEUM OF AUGUSTUS

VIA CONDOTTI

SPANISH STEPS

CAPUCHIN CRYPT

VIA VENETO

PONTE CAVOUR

VIA DUE MACELLI

VIA SISTINA

Piazza Barberini

Barberini

V. XX SETTEMBRE

VIA DELLA SCROFA

Piazza Parlamento

PARLIAMENT

VIA DEL CORSO

SABINA MURATTE

VIA DEL TRITONE

VIA 4 FONTANE

To Termini Station

PALAZZO DEL QUIRINALE

TREVI FOUNTAIN

400 Meters

400 Yards

To Piazza Venezia

To Pantheon

ever, the main attraction remains the morbid crypt. You'll begin with the Crypt of the Three Skeletons (#9). The ceiling is decorated with a skeleton grasping a grim-reaper scythe and scales. The chapel's bony chandelier and the stars and floral motifs made by ribs and vertebrae are particularly inspired. Finally, look down to read the macabre, monastic, thought-provoking message that serves as the moral of the story: "What you are now, we used to be; what we are now, you will be."

▶ €8.50, daily 10:00-19:00, modest dress required, Via Veneto 27, Metro: Barberini, +39 06 8880 3695, www.cappucciniviaveneto.it.

▲▲Dolce Vita Stroll

All over the Mediterranean world, people are out strolling in the early evening in a ritual known in Italy as the *passeggiata*. Rome's *passeggiata* is both elegant (with chic people enjoying fancy window shopping in the grid of streets around the Spanish Steps) and a little crude (with young people on the prowl).

Romans' favorite place for a chic evening stroll is along Via del Corso. Join in as you walk from Piazza del Popolo (Metro: Flaminio) down a wonderfully traffic-free section of Via del Corso, and up Via Condotti to the Spanish Steps. Although busy at any hour, this area really attracts crowds from around 17:00 to 19:00 each evening (Fri and Sat are best), except on Sunday, when it occurs earlier in the afternoon.

As you stroll, you'll see shoppers, flirts, and people watchers filling this neighborhood of some of Rome's most fashionable stores. While many Italians shop online or at the mall these days, and some elegance of this street has been replaced by international chains targeting local teens, this remains a fine place to feel the pulse of Rome at twilight.

▲Spanish Steps

The wide, curving staircase, culminating with an obelisk between two Baroque church towers, is one of Rome's iconic sights. But be sure not to sit on them (€250 fine). By day, the area hosts shoppers looking for high-end fashion; on warm evenings, it attracts young people in love with the city. For more about the steps, 📖 see the Heart of Rome Walk chapter or 🎧 download my free audio tour.

Capuchin Crypt—dem bones, dem bones…

Ara Pacis—once-bloody sacrificial altar

▲▲Museo dell'Ara Pacis (Museum of the Altar of Peace)

On January 30, 9 BC, soon-to-be-emperor Augustus led a procession of priests up the steps and into this newly built "Altar of Peace." They sacrificed an animal on the altar and poured an offering of wine, thanking the gods for helping Augustus pacify barbarians abroad and rivals at home. This marked the dawn of the Pax Romana (c. AD 1-200), a golden age of good living, stability, dominance, and peace (*pax*). The Ara Pacis (AH-rah PAH-chees) hosted annual sacrifices by the emperor until the area was flooded by the Tiber River. For an idea of how high the water could get, find the measure (*idrometro*) scaling the right side of the church closest to the entrance. Buried under silt, it was abandoned and forgotten until the 16th century, when various parts were discovered and excavated. Mussolini gathered the altar's scattered parts and reconstructed them in a building here in 1938.

This simple structure has just the basics of a Roman temple: an altar for sacrifices surrounded by cubicle-like walls that enclose a consecrated space. Its well-preserved reliefs celebrate Rome's success. After a sacrifice, the altar was washed, and the blood flowed out drain holes still visible at the base of the walls.

The reliefs on the north side depict the parade of dignitaries who consecrated the altar. Augustus stands near the head (his body sliced in two vertically by missing stone), honored with a crown of laurel leaves. He's followed by a half-dozen bigwigs and priests (with spiked hats) and the man shouldering the sacrificial ax. Reliefs on the west side (near the altar's back door) celebrate Augustus' major accomplishments: peace (goddess Roma as a conquering Amazon, right side) and prosperity (fertility goddess). Imagine the altar as it once was, standing in an open field, painted in bright colors—a mingling of myth, man, and nature.

▶ *€10.50, more with special exhibits, tightwads can look in through huge windows for free, daily 9:30-19:30, last entry one hour before closing, videoguide-€7, ask about add-on virtual reality show, a long block west of Via del Corso on Via di Ara Pacis, on the east bank of the Tiber near Ponte Cavour, Metro: Spagna plus a 10-minute walk down Via dei Condotti, +39 06 0608, www.arapacis.it.*

Mausoleum of Augustus

Just east of the Ara Pacis, the mausoleum has a diameter of 285 feet and is the world's largest known circular tomb. While it's possible to prebook a ticket to go inside, it's not particularly well presented, making it extra credit for Roman architecture completists.

▶ *€5, Tue-Sun 9:00-19:00, closed Mon, shorter hours in winter, must book online far in advance, +39 06 0608, www.mausoleodiaugusto.it.*

▲▲Catacombs of Priscilla (Catacombe di Priscilla)

While most tourists and nearly all tour groups go out to the Appian Way to see the famous catacombs of San Sebastiano and San Callisto, the Catacombs of Priscilla are less commercialized and less crowded.

The Catacombs of Priscilla likely originated as underground tombs for Christians, who'd meet to worship in the wealthy Christian's home that was on this spot. You enter from a convent and explore the result of 250 years of tunneling that occurred from the second to the fifth centuries. You'll see a few thousand of the 40,000 niches carved here, along with some beautiful frescoes, including what is considered the first depiction of Mary nursing the Baby Jesus.

▶ *€8.50, Fri-Sun 9:00-12:00 & 14:00-17:00, closed Mon-Thu though it may be open during busy times, closed one random month a year—check website or call first, Via Salaria 430, +39 06 8620 6272, www.catacombepriscilla.com.*

The catacombs are on the northeast edge of the city but well served by direct buses (30 minutes from Termini or 40 minutes from Piazza Venezia) or a €15 taxi ride. From Termini, take bus #92 or #310 from Piazza Cinquecento. From Piazza Venezia, along Via del Corso or Via Barberini, take bus #63 or #83.

EAST ROME

Near Termini Train Station

While the train-station neighborhood is not atmospheric, it contains some high-powered attractions. These sights are within a 10-minute walk of the station, near Metro stops Termini and Repubblica.

▲▲▲National Museum of Rome
(Museo Nazionale Romano Palazzo Massimo alle Terme)

The National Museum's main branch, at Palazzo Massimo, houses the greatest collection of ancient Roman art anywhere, including busts of emperors and a Roman copy of the Greek *Discus Thrower*.

Boxer at Rest at the National Museum

Villa di Livia mosaics

On the ground floor, gaze eye-to-eye with the busts of famous Romans. There's Julius Caesar, who conquered Gaul, impregnated Cleopatra, and created one-man rule. His adopted son Augustus, shown wearing the hooded robes of a priest, became the first emperor. The rest of the Julio-Claudian family is a parade of shady characters—Augustus' wily wife Livia, her moody son Tiberius, and crazy Caligula, who ordered men to kneel before him as a god.

The statue of the *Boxer at Rest* shows an exhausted pugilist slumped between rounds, gasping for air. His face is scarred, his back muscles are knotted, and his hollow-eyed expression says, "I coulda been a contender."

On the first floor is the best-preserved Roman copy of the *Discus Thrower*. Caught in mid-motion, his perfect balance summed up the order the ancients saw in nature. Statues of athletes like this commonly stood in the baths, where Romans cultivated healthy bodies, minds, and social skills, hoping to lead well-rounded lives.

The second floor focuses on frescoes and mosaics that once decorated the walls and floors of Roman villas. The basement has one of the best coin collections in Europe, from the ancient Roman denar to the Italian lira to the euro.

▶ *€10, €12 combo-ticket covers three other branches—all skippable; open Tue-Sun 9:00-19:45, closed Mon, last entry one hour before closing; audioguide may be available, about 100 yards from Termini station at Largo di Villa Peretti 2, Metro: Repubblica or Termini, +39 06 3996 7700, www.museonazionaleromano.beniculturali.it.*

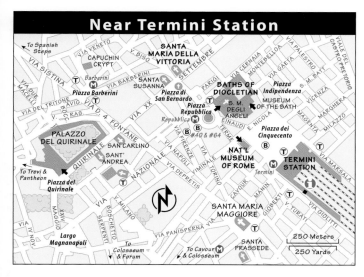

Near Termini Station

▲**Baths of Diocletian/Church of Santa Maria degli Angeli (Terme di Diocleziano/Basilica S. Maria degli Angeli)**

Of all the marvelous structures built by the Romans, their public baths were arguably the grandest, and the Baths of Diocletian were the granddaddy of them all. Built by Emperor Diocletian around AD 300 and sprawling over 30 acres—roughly five times the size of the Colosseum—these baths could cleanse 3,000 Romans at once. This impressive remnant of the ancient complex was later transformed (with help from Michelangelo) into the Church of Santa Maria degli Angeli.

The curved brick facade of today's church was once part of the *caldarium,* or steam room, of the ancient baths. Romans loved to sweat out last night's indulgences. Step into the vast and cool church. This round-domed room with an oculus (open skylight, now with modern stained glass) was once the *tepidarium*—the cooling-off room of the baths. Now enter the biggest part of the church and stand under the towering vault on the inlaid marble cross, the central hall of the baths. While the decor around you dates from the 18th century, the structure dates from the fourth century. It's the size of a football field and seven stories high.

The ceiling's crisscross arches were an architectural feat unmatched for a thousand years. The eight red granite columns are original, from ancient Rome—stand next to one and feel its five-foot girth.

From here, Romans could continue into an open-air courtyard to take a dip in the vast 32,000-square-foot swimming pool (the *frigidarium*) that paralleled this huge hall. Imagine hundreds of naked or toga-clad Romans wrestling, doing jumping jacks, singing in the baths, networking, or just milling about. Libraries, shops, bars, fast-food vendors, pedicurists, depilatories, and brothels catered to every Roman need.

▸ *Free, Mon-Sat 10:00-13:00 & 16:00-18:30, Sun until 19:00, may be open midday in summer, entrance on Piazza della Repubblica, Metro: Repubblica, www.santamariadegliangeliroma.it.*

▲Church of Santa Maria della Vittoria

This church houses Bernini's best-known statue, the swooning *St. Teresa in Ecstasy*. (Note that the church may be closed for repair work.) Inside the church, you'll find St. Teresa to the left of the altar. Teresa has just been stabbed with God's arrow of fire. Now, the angel pulls it out and watches her reaction. Teresa swoons, her eyes roll up, her hand goes limp, she parts her lips...and moans. The smiling, cherubic angel understands just how she feels. Teresa, a 16th-century Spanish nun, later talked of the "sweetness" of "this intense pain," describing her oneness with God in ecstatic, even erotic, terms.

Bernini, the master of multimedia, pulls out all the stops to make this mystical vision real. Actual sunlight pours through the alabaster windows, and bronze sunbeams shine on a marble angel holding a golden arrow. Teresa leans back on a cloud and her robe ripples from within, charged with her spiritual arousal. Bernini has created a little stage-setting of heaven. And watching from the "theater boxes" on either side are members of the family who commissioned the work.

▸ *Free (anyone collecting money at the door is not affiliated with the church), pay €0.50 for light, Mon-Sat 8:30-12:00 & 15:30-18:00, Sun 15:30-18:00, about 5 blocks northwest of Termini train station at Via XX Settembre 17, Metro: Repubblica.*

Pilgrim's Rome

In eastern Rome lie several venerable churches that Catholic pilgrims make a point of visiting. The main sights are found within a triangle

Diocletian's curved *caldarium*

The *Scala Santa*—a sacred Stairmaster

formed by Termini station, the Colosseum, and the San Giovanni Metro stop.

▲▲Church of San Giovanni in Laterano and Holy Stairs

When this church opened its doors in AD 318, it became the first place in Rome where once-persecuted Christians could finally "come out" and worship openly. Through medieval times, San Giovanni was home of the popes and the center of Catholicism until the new St. Peter's opened at the Vatican during the Renaissance.

Despite its history, the church is rather barren, having been redone in the 1600s. The spacious nave—a central hall flanked by side aisles—was the model for all basilicas to follow. The 2,000-year-old bronze doors originally hung at the ancient Senate House in the Forum. You'll see (supposed) relics of Peter and Paul and (supposed) bronze columns from the Temple of Jupiter. The bishop's chair *(cathedra)* reminds visitors that this (not St. Peter's) is the city's cathedral, presided over by the bishop of Rome—the pope.

A building near the church houses the **Holy Stairs** (Scala Santa), a staircase said to have been touched by Jesus. The 28 marble steps once stood in Pontius Pilate's residence in Jerusalem. Jesus climbed these steps on the day he was sentenced to death. In AD 326, Emperor Constantine's mother (St. Helena) brought them to Rome, where they were subsequently protected with a covering of walnut wood.

Each day, hundreds of faithful penitents climb these steps on their knees, reciting prayers. They look down through glass-covered sections to see stains from Jesus' blood. Visitors can join in or observe from the side. The steps lead to the "Holy of Holies" (Sancta Sanctorum), a chapel that, in medieval times, held important relics (now at the Vatican), and was once considered the holiest place on earth.

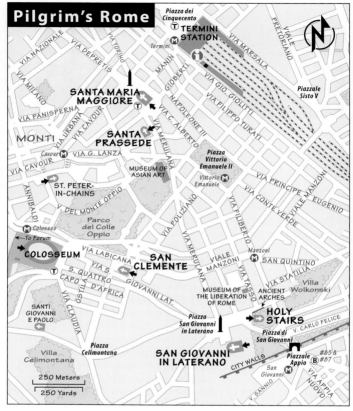

Pilgrim's Rome

► *Church and Holy Stairs—free, cloister—€3, chapel at Holy Stairs—€3.50, cloister admission plus audioguides for church and cloister—€10; church open daily 7:00-18:30, Holy Stairs open daily 6:00-13:30 & 15:00-18:30, hours may be longer during busy times; Piazza di San Giovanni in Laterano, Metro: San Giovanni or bus #87; +39 06 772 6641 (phone answered daily 8:00-13:00), www.scala-santa.com.*

▲Church of Santa Maria Maggiore

One of Rome's oldest (AD 432), simplest, and best-preserved churches, Santa Maria Maggiore was a rare oasis of order in the days when Rome was falling around it. The church is dedicated to Holy Mary, the mother of Christ, and pilgrims come to kneel before an urn containing pieces of wood from Jesus' manger (in a lighted niche under the altar). Some of Rome's best-surviving (if hard-to-see) mosaics line the nave (bring binoculars).

The church has a glorious altar of precious stones (left transept) as well as the humble floor tomb of the artist Bernini (right of the altar). In the right transept is a monument to the man who rebuilt Rome in the 16th century, the energetic Pope Sixtus V. Or was it Fiftus VI?

▶ Free, daily 7:00-18:45, Piazza di Santa Maria Maggiore, Metro: Termini or Vittorio Emanuele, +39 06 6988 6800, www.vatican.va (search for "Santa Maria Maggiore").

▲Church of San Clemente

Here, like nowhere else, you'll enjoy the layers of Rome. A 12th-century basilica sits atop a fourth-century Christian basilica, which sits atop a second-century Mithraic temple and some even earlier Roman buildings.

On the street level, you enter the 12th-century church, featuring original mosaics (in the apse) of Christ on the cross, surrounded by doves, animals, and a Tree of Life. The message: All life springs from God in Christ.

Next, descend to a fourth-century church. A faded fresco shows St. Clement holding a secret Mass for persecuted Christians, when he's suddenly arrested. As they try to drag him away, a man yells in the early Italian inscription, "Fili dele pute, traite!... You sons of bitches, pull!"

Finally, descend one more floor, to the dark, dank remains of the pagan cult of Mithras. Worshippers—men only—huddled on the benches of this low-ceilinged room. The room was a microcosm of the universe—the ceiling was once covered with stars, and the small shafts let priests follow the movements of the heavens. A carved altar shows the god Mithras, in a billowing cape, running his sword through a sacred bull. The blood spills out, bringing life to the world. Mithras' fans gathered here to eat a ritual meal celebrating the triumph of light and life over darkness and death.

▶ Upper church—free, lower church—€12, cheaper online, both open

Mon-Sat 10:00-12:30 & 15:00-17:30, Sun 12:00-17:30, Via Labicana 95, Metro: Colosseo or bus #87, +39 06 774 0021, www.basilicasanclemente. com.

TRASTEVERE AND NEARBY

Trastevere (trahs-TAY-veh-ray) is a colorful neighborhood with a medieval-village feel across (*tras*) the Tiber (*Tevere*) River. The action unwinds to the chime of the church bells. This former working-class area is becoming trendy, but it's still as close to the "real Rome" as you can get. There are no must-see tourist sights, but it's a fun people scene, especially at night, when it's a great place for dinner. For a neighborhood walk, 🎧 download my free Rick Steves audio tour of Trastevere.

To reach Trastevere by foot from Capitoline Hill, cross the Tiber on Ponte Cestio (over Isola Tiberina). You can also take tram #8 from Piazza Venezia or Largo Argentina, or bus #H from Termini and Piazza della Repubblica to Piazza Belli. From the Vatican (Piazza Risorgimento), take bus #23.

▲Church of Santa Maria in Trastevere

One of Rome's oldest church sites, a basilica was erected here in the fourth century, when Christianity was legalized. It is said to have been the first church in Rome dedicated to the Virgin Mary. The structure you see today dates mainly from the 12th century. Its portico (covered area just outside the door) is decorated with fascinating fragments of stone—many of them lids from catacomb burial niches—and filled with early Christian symbolism. Out front on Piazza di Santa Maria, an impressive 17th-century fountain stands on the same spot where locals have been drawing water since Roman times. The piazza is the neighborhood meeting place, where kids play soccer, layabouts lay about the fountain steps, and people crowd the outdoor restaurants.

▶ *Free, Mon-Fri 7:30-20:30, Sat until 21:00, Sun until 20:00, shorter hours with midday closure in Aug.*

▲Villa Farnesina

Here's a unique opportunity to see a sumptuous Renaissance villa in Rome decorated with Raphael paintings. It was built in the early 1500s for the richest man in Renaissance Europe, Sienese banker Agostino

Trastevere—a bit rougher but more real

Santa Maria in Trastevere—mosaics

Chigi. Kings and popes of the day depended on generous loans from Chigi, whose bank had more than 100 branches in places as far-flung as London and Cairo. His villa here in Rome was the meeting place of aristocrats, artists, beautiful women, and philosophers. It's a quick visit (there are only four main rooms).

Architect Baldassare Peruzzi's design—a U-shaped building with wings enfolding what used to be a vast garden—successfully blended architecture and nature in a way that both ancient and Renaissance Romans loved. Orchards and flower beds flowed down in terraces from the palace to the riverbanks. Later construction of modern embankments and avenues robbed the garden of its grandeur, leaving it with a more melancholy charm. Inside, cavorting gods and goddesses cover the walls and ceilings, most famously Raphael's depiction of the sea nymph Galatea.

▶ *€10, includes audioguide; Mon-Sat 9:00-14:00, closed Sun except open 9:00-17:00 on second Sun of month; guided visit in English on Sat at 10:00; across the river from Campo de' Fiori, a short walk from Ponte Sisto and a block behind the river at Via della Lungara 230; +39 06 6802 7268, www.villafarnesina.it.*

SOUTH ROME

In South Rome you'll find ancient ruins, including the famous Appian Way with its underground catacombs. There's the gritty-but-trendy neighborhood of Testaccio. South of that is a major pilgrimage church, and farther still is the eerie suburb of the future built by Mussolini, called E.U.R. To find these sights, see the foldout map.

Ancient Appian Way and Southeastern Rome

Southeast of the city center lie several ancient sites that make the trek here worthwhile.

▲Appian Way and Catacombs

The famous ancient Roman road offers three attractions: the old road itself, lined with crumbling tombs and monuments; the underground Christian catacombs; and the peaceful atmosphere of pine and cypress trees. Concentrate on the sight-packed stretch of road between the Tomb of Cecilia Metella and the Domine Quo Vadis Church.

The Appian Way once ran 430 miles from Rome to the Adriatic port of Brindisi, the gateway to Greece. After Spartacus' slave revolt was suppressed (71 BC), the road was lined with 6,000 crucified slaves as a warning. Today you can walk (or bike) some stretches of the road, rattling over original paving stones and past mile markers. The two most impressive pagan sights are the ruins of the **Tomb of Cecilia Metella** (a massive cylindrical burial place for a rich noblewoman) and the **Circus of Maxentius** (a once-grand chariot racetrack).

When the Christian faith permeated Rome, Christians were buried along the Appian Way in labyrinthine underground tunnels called catacombs. Legends say that early Christians lived in the catacombs to escape persecution, but that's not true.

The two major catacombs—**San Sebastiano and San Callisto**—are a few hundred yards apart. At either place, a guide leads you underground to see burial niches (but no bones), faded frescoes, memorial chapels to saints, Christian symbols (doves, fish, anchors), and graffiti by early Christian tag artists. Both catacombs are quite similar, so pick one to tour.

Appian Way—site of the catacombs

Testaccio—ancient pyramid and city gate

The tiny Domine Quo Vadis Church marks the spot where Peter, fleeing Rome, saw a vision of Christ. Peter asked Jesus, "Lord, where are you going?" (*"Domine quo vadis?"* in Latin), to which Christ replied, "I am going to Rome to be crucified again." The vision shamed Peter into returning to the wicked city.

▶ ***The Tomb of Cecilia Metella:*** *€10 for My Appia Card; open Tue-Sun 9:00-19:00, closes earlier Oct-March, closed Mon year-round; +39 06 3996 7700, www.coopculture.it.*

Circus of Maxentius: *Free, Tue-Sun 10:00-16:00, closed Mon, www.villadimassenzio.it.*

Catacombs of San Sebastiano: *€8.50, daily 10:00-17:00, closed Dec, Via Appia Antica 136, +39 06 785 0350, www.catacombe.org.*

Catacombs of San Callisto: *€8.50, Thu-Tue 9:00-12:00 & 14:00-17:00, closed Wed and late Jan-late Feb, Via Appia Antica 110, +39 06 513 0151, www.catacombe.roma.it.*

To get there and back, I recommend this route: Take a taxi (€20) or bus (#660 from the Colli Albani Metro stop) to the Tomb of Cecilia Metella. Walk the Appian Way to the Catacombs of San Sebastiano. From there, avoid the most-trafficked stretch of road by taking the peaceful pedestrian path (enter through the arch at #126), which leads to the Catacombs of San Callisto and continues to the Domine Quo Vadis Church. From there, catch bus #118 to the Circo Massimo Metro stop. You're back in central Rome—"Quo vadis," pilgrim?

Baths of Caracalla (Terme di Caracalla)

Inaugurated by Emperor Caracalla in AD 216, this massive bath complex—supplied by its own branch of an aqueduct—could accommodate 1,600 visitors at a time. Today it's just a shell—a huge shell—with all its sculptures and most of its mosaics moved to museums. You'll see a two-story roofless brick building surrounded by a garden, bordered by ruined walls. Two large exercise rooms flank the former swimming pool. The baths functioned until Goths severed the aqueducts in the sixth century. In modern times, grand operas are performed here during the summer (see www.operaroma.it).

▶ *€8, Mon 9:00-14:00, Tue-Sun 9:00 until one hour before sunset, last entry one hour before closing, audioguide-€5, +39 06 3996 7700, www.coopculture.it. Metro: Circo Massimo, then a 5-minute walk* *south along Via delle Terme di Caracalla; bus #714 from Termini train station.*

Testaccio

In the creative, postindustrial Testaccio neighborhood, you can spend a pleasant hour exploring several fascinating but lesser sights near the Piramide Metro stop.

Long a working-class neighborhood, Testaccio has gone trendy-bohemian. Visitors wander through an awkward mix of hipster and proletarian worlds, not noticing—but perhaps sensing—the "Keep Testaccio for the Testaccians" graffiti.

Monte Testaccio, a small hill, is actually a 115-foot-tall ancient trash pile made of broken testae—broken pots. Two thousand years ago, old pottery jars were discarded here, and slowly, Rome's lowly eighth hill was built. Today, the hill is surrounded by a mix of gritty car-repair places and trendy bars. For the full experience, be here after 21:00, when the nightlife kicks in.

The **Pyramid of Gaius Cestius** stands next to the Piramide Metro stop. This 90-foot-tall marble-over-brick structure was built around 30 BC, at a time when Mark Antony was wooing Cleopatra, and exotic Egyptian styles were in vogue.

Nearby is the **Porta San Paolo,** a gate in the 12-mile Aurelian Wall (third century) that once encircled the city. Inside the gate is a tiny (free) museum, the Museo della Via Ostiense, displaying models of Ostia Antica, Rome's ancient port (Tue-Sun 9:00-13:00, closed Mon).

The **Protestant Cemetery** is a peaceful, tomb-filled park. Upon entering, head 90 degrees left to find the tomb of English poet John Keats (1795-1821), in the far corner. The tomb of fellow poet Percy Shelley (1792-1822) is straight ahead from the entrance, up the hill, at the base of the stubby tower. Both Romantic poets came on the Grand Tour and—"captivated by the fatal charms of Rome," as Shelley wrote—never left (€5 suggested donation, Mon-Sat 9:00-17:00, Sun until 13:00, www.cemeteryrome.it).

South of Testaccio

You can ride the Metro to the Montemartini Museum and St. Paul's Outside the Walls, but to stay above ground, buses #23 and #769 run along Via Ostiense from the Piramide Metro stop to the museum (stop: Ostiense/Garbatella) and the church (stop: Viale S. Paolo).

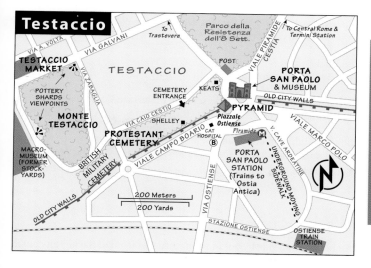

▲Montemartini Museum
(Musei Capitolini Centrale Montemartini)

This museum houses a dreamy collection of 400 ancient statues, set evocatively in a classic 1932 electric power plant, among generators and *Metropolis*-type cast-iron machinery. While the art is not as famous as the collections you'll see downtown, the effect is fun and memorable—and you won't encounter a single tourist.

▶ €10, Tue-Sun 9:00-19:00, closed Mon, look for red banner marking Via Ostiense 106, a short walk from Metro: Garbatella, +39 06 0608, www. centralemontemartini.org.

▲St. Paul's Outside the Walls
(Basilica San Paolo Fuori le Mura)

This was the last major construction project of Imperial Rome (AD 380) and the largest church in Christendom until St. Peter's. The interior, lit by alabaster windows, is vast—if a bit sterile. What is believed to be the sarcophagus of St. Paul is visible under the altar.

▶ *Free, open daily 7:00-18:30, modest dress code enforced, café, Via*

Ostiense 186, Metro: Basilica San Paolo, +39 06 6988 0800, www. basilicasanpaolo.org.

E.U.R.

The 1930s-era planned city built by Italy's dictator Benito Mussolini was designed to show off the wonders of his fascist society. E.U.R.'s key landmark is the lone skyscraper understandably nicknamed the "Square Colosseum." Today, E.U.R. (pronounced AY-oor) is worth a trip for its Museum of Roman Civilization (may be closed for renovation), its Italian modernism (for architecture buffs), and to see what our world might look like if Hitler and Mussolini had won the war.

► *To reach E.U.R., get off at Metro stop Magliana for the "Square Colosseum," or Metro stop Fermi for the Museum of Roman Civilization.*

NEAR ROME

An hour or two ride by bus or train can get you out of the big-city bustle to some peaceful sights. Think of these as day trips, as they'll consume most of a sightseeing day.

▲▲Ostia Antica

The ancient Roman port city of Ostia is similar to the famous ruins of Pompeii but a lot closer and less touristed. Wandering around, you'll see ruined warehouses, apartment flats, mansions, shopping arcades, and baths that served a once-thriving port of 60,000 people.

Enter through the main city gate (Porta Romana) and walk down the long, straight main drag (Decumanus Maximus), past once-vast warehouses. Pop into the well-preserved Theater, which could seat 4,000 and is still used today. Behind the stage, explore the Square of the Guilds, once lined with more than 60 offices. The sidewalks have mosaics advertising their lines of business—grain silos, an elephant for ivory traders, boats for ship-makers, and the symbol of Ostia itself, a lighthouse.

Continuing down main street, detour right down Via dei Molini, and find the mill (Molino), the tavern (Insula of the Thermopolium), and a typical apartment house (the Insula of the Paintings). Ostia's working class lived in cramped, noisy multistory buildings, with no plumbing, heat, or kitchens—they survived on takeout food.

The main street spills into the town's main square, or Forum, dominated by the Capitolium temple, dedicated to the trinity of Jupiter, Juno, and Minerva. Now just a brick core, the temple was originally huge, fronted with columns and faced with gleaming white marble.

Near the Forum Baths (Terme del Foro), find the latrine. Yes, those 20 holes are toilets. Rushing water below the seats did the flushing. Privacy? Even today there's no Italian word for it.

▶ *€12, Tue-Sun 8:30-19:00, shorter hours off-season, closed Mon year-round, last entry one hour before closing. +39 06 5635 0215, www.ostiaantica.beniculturali.it. ∩ A free Rick Steves audio tour is available.*

Getting There: *From Rome's Piramide Metro stop (also a train station), catch any train headed toward Lido—they all stop at Ostia Antica. A single Metro ticket covers the one-way train ride. Arriving at Ostia Antica, leave the train station, cross the blue skybridge, and walk straight down Via della Stazione di Ostia Antica to reach the parking lot and entrance.*

▲Tivoli: The Villa d'Este and Hadrian's Villa

At the edge of the Sabine Hills, 18 miles east of Rome, sits the pleasant medieval hill town of Tivoli. Today, it's famous for two very different country estates: the Villa d'Este (a 16th-century mansion with playful fountains) and Hadrian's Villa (the ruins of the Roman emperor's palatial retreat).

The Villa d'Este: Cardinal Ippolito d'Este, a sophisticated lover of luxury, built this personal pleasure palace in the 1550s. It's a watery wonderland—a mansion with terraced gardens and fountains on a cool hill with breath-catching views. Its design and statuary were inspired by (and looted from) the ancient villa of Hadrian.

E.U.R.'s "Square Colosseum"

Ostia Antica—Pompeii without the crowds

Hadrian's Villa, outside Rome—where the emperor retreated to ponder his vast empire

The Villa d'Este's star attraction is hundreds of Baroque fountains, most of which are still gravity-powered. The Aniene River, frazzled into countless threads, weaves its way entertainingly through the villa. At the bottom of the garden, the exhausted little streams once again team up to make a sizable river.

Hike through the gardens, and then enjoy the restaurant, opportunely placed on the highest terrace to catch cool afternoon sea breezes.

Hadrian's Villa: Emperor Hadrian (ruled AD 117-138) built this country residence as an escape from the heat of Rome and the pressures of court life. The Spanish-born Hadrian ruled at the peak of the Roman Empire, when it stretched from England to the Euphrates and encompassed countless diverse cultures. Hadrian—a great traveler—had personally visited many of the lands he ruled. At Tivoli, he created a microcosm of his empire, re-creating famous structures from around the world—an Egyptian-style canal, a Greek-style stoa, and so on. The Teatro Marittimo is a circular palace set on an artificial island. Here Hadrian could sit, at the symbolic center of his vast empire, and ponder what might become of it.

▶ ***Villa d'Este:*** *€13, Tue-Sun 8:30-19:45, Mon from 14:00, closes as early* as 17:00 off-season, last entry one hour before closing, +39 0774 335 850, www.levillae.com.

Hadrian's Villa (Villa Adriana): €10, daily 8:30-19:00 in summer, closes as early as 17:00 off-season, last entry 1.5 hours before closing, +39 0774 382 733, www.levillae.com.

Getting to Tivoli: From Rome's Metro stop Ponte Mammolo, take the local blue Cotral bus to Tivoli (45 minutes, 2/hour, buy bus tickets at Metro station bar/newsstand). In Tivoli, the Villa d'Este is in the center of town near the Tivoli bus stop. To continue to Hadrian's Villa (2.5 miles outside Tivoli), catch the gray "CAT" city bus #4 or #4X at the same bus stop (buy round-trip tickets at tobacco shop/newsstand).

Activities

Rome has wowed visitors with dazzling spectacles for thousands of years. While gladiators and chariot races are a thing of the past, this chapter covers activities—tours, shopping, and entertainment—that you can enjoy today.

To get oriented, consider splicing Rome's sights together with the help of a group walking tour or private local guide.

Whatever your taste or budget, Rome is great for shoppers. It's equally fun to gawk at ultra-chic designer stores near the Spanish Steps or browse through typical street markets scattered across the city.

At night, stroll Rome's streets and piazzas like a local, take in a sound-and-light show among ancient ruins, or listen to opera where it was invented. For the ultimate Roman experience, consider going to a soccer game.

TOURS

To sightsee on your own, 🎧 download free audio tours of my Heart of Rome, Jewish Ghetto, and Trastevere neighborhood walks, and my tours of the Pantheon, Colosseum, Roman Forum, St. Peter's Basilica, Vatican Museums, Sistine Chapel, and Ostia Antica.

On Foot

Local Guides: Private guides are good but pricey (around €180 for a three-hour tour). I've worked with and enjoyed each of these licensed independent local guides: **Carla Zaia** (carlaromeguide@gmail.com); **Cristina Giannicchi** (+39 338 111 4573, www.crisromanguide.com); **Sara Magister** (a.magister@iol.it); **Giovanna Terzulli** (gioterzulli@gmail.com); **Alessandra Mazzoccoli** (www.romeandabout.com); and **Massimiliano Canneto** (massicanneto@gmail.com). **Francesca Caruso**, who works almost full-time with my tours when in Rome, has contributed generously to this book (www.francescacaruso.com, francescainroma@gmail.com); she offers private tours for €300/half-day. Popular with my readers, Francesca understandably books up quickly; if she's busy, she'll recommend one of her colleagues.

Walking Tour Companies: Rome has many highly competitive tour companies, each offering a series of themed walks through various slices of the city. Three-hour guided walks generally cost €25-30 per person. These companies are each well established, creative, and competitive, with their various tours explained on their websites. Each offers a 10 percent discount with most online bookings for Rick Steves travelers: **Walks of Italy** (RS%—enter "RICKSTEVESROME10," US +1 888 683 8670, +39 06 9480 4888, www.walksofitaly.com); **Europe Odyssey** (RS%, +39 06 8854 2416, mobile +39 388 121 5318, www.europeodyssey. com, Rahul); **Through Eternity** (RS%—look for "Group Tours Rome" and enter "RICKSTEVES," US +1 800 267 7581, www.througheternity.com, office@througheternity.com, Rob); **The Roman Guy** (RS%—enter "ricksteves," ask about e-bike tours, US +1 888 290 5595, theromanguy.com, Sean Finelli); and **Miles & Miles Private Tours,** described under "Car & Minibus Tours," next, also offers walking tours (www. milesandmiles.net). They are a great value, especially if a car is used.

Guides bring ancient ruins back to life.

Roman markets—always colorful

On Wheels

Car and Minibus Tours: Miles & Miles Private Tours has good English-speaking Italian driver/guides and fine air-conditioned cars and minibuses. Their basic line-up for groups of up to eight people includes a five-hour "History and Fun" tour (€350, RS%—mention Rick Steves when booking direct, then show this book; +39 331 466 4900, www. milesandmiles.net, info@milesandmiles.net).

Hop-On, Hop-Off Bus Tours: Several agencies run hop-on, hop-off, double-decker bus tours that make the same 90-minute, eight-stop loop through the traffic-congested town center with about four pick-ups at each stop per hour. Buses provide an easy way to see the city from above the congestion (choose open or with canopy), but the lazy recorded narration does little more than identify the sightseeing icons you drive by. You can join one at any stop (pay as you board; usually around €20; Termini station and Piazza Venezia are handy hubs).

Car and Driver Service: Autoservizi Monti Concezio offers private cars or minibuses with driver/guides (car-€40/hour, minibus-€45/hour, 3-hour minimum for city sightseeing, transfers between cities are more expensive, mobile +39 335 636 5907 or +39 349 674 5643, info@tourservicemonti.it).

SHOPPING

Rome is a wonderful city to shop in. Even if you're not aiming to buy anything, exploring popular shopping areas provides a break from stressful, clogged tourist sights and an excuse to lose yourself on a charming street.

Traditionally, shops are open from roughly 9:00 to 13:00 and from 15:30 or 16:00 to 19:00 or 19:30. They're often closed on Sundays, summer Saturday afternoons, and winter Monday mornings. But in the city center, many now stay open through lunch (generally 10:00-19:00).

If all you need are souvenirs, any gift shop will do. Otherwise, stop at a department store, scout near the Vatican or in the Jewish Ghetto for religious items, hit the flea market and produce markets, or—if you're in a pinch—pick up some mementos at the airport on your way out of town.

Shopping Neighborhoods

The city's top shopping areas are all equally good, but each has a different flavor. The **"Heart of Rome"** near Piazza Navona and Campo de' Fiori is heavy on antiques and home furnishings, but you can find souvenirs here as well. The **Jewish Ghetto** is lined with cute boutiques, food stands, kosher butchers, and a few Judaica shops. The **Monti district,** convenient to the ancient sites, is a hipster neighborhood with gourmet foodie shops and funky boutiques alongside traditional neighborhood stores. The area known as the **"Shopping Triangle"** along Via del Corso and near the Spanish Steps has big international chains along with some very famous designers.

Department Stores

The shopping complex under Termini train station is a convenient place to peruse clothes, bags, shoes, and perfume at several major Italian chain stores (most open daily 8:00-22:00).

A good upscale department store is **La Rinascente** (Via del Tritone 61). Besides deluxe brands, it has a fine design section with great and often affordable ideas for gifts, a magnificent rooftop terrace for a romantic *aperitivo,* good restaurants, free bathrooms, and a section of an ancient aqueduct in the basement (worth a quick visit). You'll find another branch on Piazza Fiume (east of the Borghese Gallery).

The **Galleria Alberto Sordi** is an elegant 19th-century "mall" (across from Piazza Colonna). **UPIM** is a popular midrange department store (many branches, including inside Termini train station, Via Nazionale 111, and Piazza Santa Maria Maggiore). **Oviesse/OVS,** a cheap clothing outlet, is near the Vatican Museums (on the corner of Via Candia and Via Mocenigo, Metro: Cipro) and also near Piazza Barberini (Via del Tritone 172, Metro: Barberini).

Street Markets

Flea Markets: For antiques and fleas, the granddaddy of markets is the **Porta Portese** *mercato delle pulci* (flea market). This Sunday-morning market is long and spindly, running between the actual Porta Portese (a gate in the old town wall) and the Trastevere train station. For something a bit hipper, visit the weekend **Mercato Monti** in the Monti district. This flea market has an emphasis on vintage clothes and housewares and up-and-coming designers (Sat-Sun 10:00-20:00, closed July-Aug, Hotel Palatino, Via Leonina 46, Metro: Cavour, www.mercatomonti.com).

Open-Air Produce Markets: For a fun and colorfully authentic experience, wander through the easygoing neighborhood produce markets that clog certain streets and squares every morning (7:00-13:30) except Sunday. Consider the huge **Mercato Trionfale** (three blocks north of Vatican Museums at Via Andrea Doria). Another great food market is the **Mercato Esquilino** (near Termini station at Via Filippo Turati, Metro: Vittorio Emanuele). The covered **Mercato di Testaccio** sells produce and housewares and is a hit with photographers and people-watchers (Metro: Piramide). Smaller but equally charming slices of everyday Roman life are at markets on these streets and squares: **Piazza delle Coppelle** (near the Pantheon), **Via Balbo** (off Via Nazionale), and **Via della Pace** (near Piazza Navona). And **Campo de' Fiori,** despite having become quite touristy, is still a fun scene.

VAT and Customs

Getting a VAT Refund: If you purchase more than €155 worth of goods at a single store, you may be eligible to get a refund of the 22 percent Value-Added Tax (VAT). Get more details from the merchant or see RickSteves.com/vat.

Customs for American Shoppers: You can take home $800 worth of items per person duty-free, once every 31 days. You can bring in one liter of alcohol duty-free. For details on allowable goods, customs rules, and duty rates, visit Help.cbp.gov.

ENTERTAINMENT AND NIGHTLIFE

For most visitors, the best entertainment in Rome is simply to grab a gelato and join in the *passeggiata,* the evening stroll through the medieval lanes that connect Rome's romantic, floodlit squares and fountains. Head for Piazza Navona, the Pantheon, Campo de' Fiori, Trevi Fountain, the Spanish Steps, Via del Corso, Trastevere (around the Santa Maria in Trastevere Church), or Monte Testaccio.

Of course, there's much more going on. For the current listings of concerts, operas, dance, and films, check these English-language websites: www.wantedinrome.com and www.angloinfo.com.

Music

Contemporary Music: The Auditorium (Auditorium Parco della Musica) is where many Romans go just for the scene—music store, restaurants, cafés, and concerts (€20-60 tickets, check availability in advance—concerts often sell out, Viale Pietro de Coubertin 30, take Metro to Flaminio and then catch tram #2 to Apollodoro, from there it's a 5-minute walk east, just beyond the elevated road, tram/metro runs until 23:30, box office +39 02 6006 0900, www.auditorium.com).

Classical Music and Opera: The Teatro dell'Opera has an active schedule of opera and classical concerts (tickets from €25, online reservations encouraged, box office takes phone reservations beginning 5 days prior at +39 06 481 7003; Piazza Beniamino Gigli 7, a block off Via Nazionale, Metro: Repubblica; www.operaroma.it). Opera da Camera di Roma is a tourist-oriented, greatest-hits-of-opera performance in various smaller venues around Rome. Buy the cheapest tickets and request the Rick Steves upgrade (RS%—use the code "RickSteves"; check schedule and book on their website, +39 320 530 7112, www.operadacameradiroma.com).

Jazz: Alexanderplatz is the venerable club in town (Via Ostia 9, Metro: Ottaviano, +39 06 8678 1296, www.alexanderplatzjazz.com). **TramJazz** combines dinner, music, and a journey through the city in a vintage cable car for a mostly local crowd (€75, daily at 21:00, 3 hours, leaves from Piazza di Porta Maggiore—reached by tram #5 or #14 from Termini station, book well ahead, www.tramjazz.com).

Rome's romantic squares are best at night.

Other Late-Night Fun

Sound-and-Light Shows: The Imperial Forums area hosts two atmospheric and inspirational sound-and-light shows that bring the ancient rubble to life. Consider one or both of the similar and adjacent evening experiences—the Caesar's Forum Stroll and the Forum of Augustus Show. You'll spend about an hour with a headphone dialed to English, listening to an artfully crafted narration synced with projections on ancient walls, columns, and porticos (€15, both for €25, nightly mid-April–mid-Nov—bring your warmest coat, confirm the schedule and prebook on website, shows can sell out on busy weekends, +39 06 0608, www.viaggioneifori.it). If you plan to see both, do Caesar first and allow 80 minutes between starting times.

Movies: Movies in their original language are scarce in Rome, but not impossible to come by (look for v.o.—*versione originale*). For a list of what's showing in English, check RomeReview.com. The most reliable theater for English-language films is the Nuovo Olimpia (3 blocks north of Piazza Colonna, just off Via del Corso at Via in Lucina 16, +39 06 686 1068).

Bars and Nightspots: Here are some fun neighborhoods worth exploring after dark. The **Heart of Rome,** near the Pantheon, is touristy but delightful. The monuments—especially the Pantheon and Trevi

Become a fanatic soccer fan for a day.

Fountain—are magically floodlit at night. **North Rome,** near the Spanish Steps and Via del Corso, is a glitzy zone bustling after dark. For many, just hanging out around the Spanish Steps is enough to fill an evening. Near the Colosseum and Forum, in **Monti,** the best plan is to pop the top off a brew and hang out at the fountain on Piazza della Madonna dei Monti. **Trastevere** is a youthful district where students and younger tourists drink beer, eat late-night pizza-by-the-slice, and lick cones of gelato as they prowl the cobbles. In South Rome, some find the **Testaccio** district a bit seedy after dark, but young Romans don't seem to mind. Monte Testaccio, once an ancient trash heap, is now a small hill whose cool caves house funky restaurants and trendy clubs.

Soccer

Rome has a special passion for soccer. It has two teams, Roma (representing the city) and Lazio (the region), and the rivalry is fanatical. Both teams call the Olympic Stadium home, so you can catch a game most weekends from September to May (Metro line A to Flaminio, then catch tram #2 to the end of the line, Piazza Mancini, and cross the bridge to the stadium). It's best to buy tickets in advance through the teams' official websites, at www.sportsevents365.com, or via resale websites such as StubHub.

Sleeping

Choosing the right neighborhood in Rome is as important as choosing the right hotel. All my recommended accommodations are in safe areas convenient to sightseeing. Central hotels near **ancient Rome** are close to the Colosseum and Roman Forum (with the trendy Monti area nearby). The most romantic ambience is in neighborhoods near the **Pantheon,** which encompass the Campo de' Fiori and the Jewish Ghetto. Hotels near **Vatican City** put St. Peter's and the Vatican Museums at your doorstep. The **Termini train station** neighborhood is a hub of good, midrange hotels that are handy for public transit and services, although the area is not particularly charming. Finally, the bohemian **Trastevere** neighborhood is a good choice for living like a Roman (or a young American expat) when in Rome for a few days.

I like places that are clean, central, relatively quiet at night, reasonably priced, friendly, small enough to have a hands-on owner or manager, and run with a respect for Italian traditions. If I can find a place with most of these features, it's a keeper.

Rome Hotels

My recommendations include everything from €25 bunks to deluxe €350 doubles, although most of the hotels listed here cluster around €170. Cheaper doubles (around €100) are available, but I favor these pricier options because intense Rome is easier to enjoy with a welcoming oasis to call home.

A typical €170 double room will have one double bed or two twins. At this price, the room probably has air-conditioning (a must in summer). Elevators are common, though small, and some older buildings still lack them. You may have to climb a flight of stairs to reach the elevator (if so, you can ask the front desk for help carrying your bags up).

Italian hotels typically include breakfast in their room prices—a simple continental buffet with (at its most generous) bread, croissants, ham, cheese, yogurt, and unlimited *caffè latte*. Rome charges a hotel tax of €3-7 per person, per night, which is typically not included in the prices in this book.

Some hotels can add an extra bed (for a small charge) to turn a double into a triple; some offer larger rooms for four or more people (I call these "family rooms" in the listings).

Making Reservations

Reserve your rooms as soon as you've pinned down your travel dates. For busy national holidays, it's wise to reserve far in advance. Book your room directly via email or phone, or through the hotel's official website.

Here's what the hotelier wants to know:
- Type(s) of room(s) you want and number of guests
- Number of nights you'll stay
- Arrival and departure dates, written European-style as day/month/year (for example, 18/06/24 or 18 June 2024);
- Special requests (en suite bathroom, cheapest room, twin beds vs. double bed, quiet room)
- Applicable discounts (such as a Rick Steves discount, cash discount, or promotional rate)

Most places will request a credit-card number to hold your room. If the hotel's website doesn't have a secure form where you can enter the number directly, share this info via a phone call. If you must cancel, it's courteous—and smart—to do so with as much notice as possible. Cancellation policies can be strict; read the fine print. Always call or email to reconfirm your room reservation a few days in advance.

Sleep Code

Dollar signs reflect average rates for a standard double room with breakfast in high season.

$$$$	**Splurge:** Most rooms over €170
$$$	**Pricier:** €130-170
$$	**Moderate:** €90-130
$	**Budget:** €50-90
¢	**Backpacker:** Under €50
RS%	**Rick Steves discount**

Unless otherwise noted, credit cards are accepted, hotel staff speak basic English, and free Wi-Fi is available. If the listing includes RS%, request a Rick Steves discount.

Budget Tips

It's common for hotels in Rome to cut their prices up to 50 percent in the off-season, although prices at hostels and cheaper hotels won't fluctuate much. Room rates are lowest in sweltering August. To get the best rates, book directly with the hotel. Some hotels extend a discount to those who pay cash or stay longer than three nights. And some accommodations offer a special discount for Rick Steves readers, indicated in this guidebook by the abbreviation "RS%."

Besides hotels, there are cheaper alternatives. B&Bs can offer good-value accommodations in excellent locations. A short-term rental—whether an apartment, a house, or a room in a private residence—is a popular alternative, especially if you plan to settle in one location for several nights. Websites such as Airbnb, FlipKey, Booking.com, and VRBO let you browse a wide range of properties. In Rome, also try Cross-Pollinate.com.

NEAR ANCIENT ROME

Central location, a short walk from the Colosseum and Roman Forum, near the Cavour Metro stop.

$$$$ Hotel Lancelot Elegant feel at a fair price, family-run, quiet and safe, air-con, elevator, wheelchair accessible.

Via Capo d'Africa 47, +39 06 7045 0615, www.lancelothotel.com

$$$$ Nerva Boutique Hotel Tranquil with 20 small and often discounted rooms, facing the Roman Forum, RS%—use code "RICKSTEVES," air-con.

Via Tor de' Conti 3, +39 06 678 1835, www.hotelnerva.com

$$$ Hotel Paba Homey, lovingly run, two blocks from the Forum, RS%, email reservations preferred, air-con, elevator.

Via Cavour 266, second floor, +39 06 4782 4497, www.hotelpaba.com

$$ Casa Il Rosario Well-run Dominican convent, RS%—use code "ricksteves," reserve several months in advance, some rooms with air-con and others with fans, elevator, midnight curfew.

Via Sant'Agata dei Goti 10, +39 06 679 2346, www.casailrosarioroma.it

$$ Hotel Antica Locanda On a small street, stylish furnishings, rooftop terrace, air-con, no elevator.

Via del Boschetto 84, +39 06 484 894, www.anticalocandaroma.it

$$ Hotel Rosetta Homey and family-run, minimal, no lounge and no breakfast, air-con.

Via Cavour 295, +39 06 4782 3069, www.rosettahotel.com

NEAR TERMINI STATION: WEST OF THE STATION

Hotels on or near Via Firenze, a safe, handy, central, and quiet street near two Metro stops—Repubblica and Termini—and Via Nazionale (#60, #64, #70, and the #40 express).

$$$$ Hotel Cellini Feels like the guest wing of gorgeous Neoclassical palace, all the comforts and service, RS%, air-con, elevator.

Via Modena 5, third floor, +39 06 4782 5204, www.hotelcellini.it

$$$$ Hotel Modigliani Energetically run, clean, bright, minimalist, plush lounge, garden, RS%, air-con, elevator.

Via della Purificazione 42, +39 06 4281 5226, www.hotelmodigliani.com

$$$$ IQ Hotel Efficient with modern amenities, spacious, RS%, family rooms, breakfast extra, air-con, elevator.

Via Firenze 8, +39 06 488 0465, www.iqhotelroma.it

$$$ Hotel Aberdeen Combines quality and friendliness, family-run, comfy rooms, RS%—use "Rick Steves reader reservations" link, family rooms, air-con.

Via Firenze 48, +39 06 482 3920, www.hotelaberdeen.it

$$$ Hotel Oceania Peaceful, thoughtful extra touches, family atmosphere, RS%—use code "RICKSTEVES," family rooms, elevator.

Via Firenze 38, third floor, +39 06 482 4696, www.hoteloceania.it

$$ Hotel Nardizzi Americana Slightly scruffy rooms, rooftop terrace, decent value, RS%—email reservation for discount, family rooms, air-con, elevator.

Via Firenze 38, fourth floor, +39 06 488 0035, www.hotelnardizzi.it

$$ Hotel Italia Busy and handy locale, modest but comfortable rooms, RS%, family rooms, air-con, elevator.

Via Venezia 18, +39 06 482 8355, www.hotelitaliaroma.it

¢ The RomeHello Modern, quiet, comfortable, about 200 beds in doubles, triples, and dorms.

Via Torino 45, +39 06 9686 0070, www.theromehello.com

NEAR TERMINI: SOUTHWEST OF THE STATION

Good-value places near the Basilica of Santa Maria Maggiore and the Cavour Metro stop.

$$$ Hotel Raffaello Courteous and professional staff, grand 19th-century building, generous public spaces, family rooms, air-con, elevator.

Via Urbana 3, +39 06 488 4342, www.hotelraffaello.it

$$ Hotel Domus Nova Bethlem Owned by the Oblate Sisters of Baby Jesus; spacious, pristine, modest yet classy rooms; RS%, air-con, elevator.

Via Cavour 85A, +39 06 4782 4414, www.dnbhotel.com

$$ Hotel Montreal Basic, on big and noisy street, RS%, family rooms, air-con, elevator, small garden terrace.

Via Carlo Alberto 4, +39 06 445 7797, www.hotelmontrealroma.it

$ Suore di Santa Elisabetta Heavenly Polish-run convent, serene garden, roof terrace, fans but no air-con, elevator for top floors, Wi-Fi in lounge only, 23:00 curfew.

Via dell'Olmata 9, +39 06 488 8271, www.csse-roma.com

NEAR TERMINI: NORTHEAST OF THE STATION

Cheapest beds in town, just beyond Termini train station.

$$ Hotel Astoria Garden Modern and comfortable, beautiful lemon-tree garden, welcoming refuge, air-con, elevator.

Via V. Bachelet 6, +39 06 446 9908, www.hotelastoriagarden.it

$ The Beehive Cheap, clean, comfy, some rooms with shared baths, dorm in main building, air-con in some rooms, breakfast extra, private garden terrace.

Via Marghera 8, +39 06 4470 4553, www.the-beehive.com

$ Hotel Robinson On interior courtyard, small and simple rooms, RS%—includes breakfast and air-con when you pay in cash.

Via Milazzo 3, +39 06 491 423, www.hotelrobinsonrome.com

¢ YellowSquare Hostel Hip yet sane, party hostel, loads of activities, great dorms.

Via Palestro 44, +39 06 446 3554, https://yellowsquare.it/roma

PANTHEON NEIGHBORHOOD: NEAR THE PANTHEON

Pedestrian-friendly heart of ancient Rome, a bit distant from public transportation arteries.

$$$$ Hotel Nazionale Four-star landmark in 16th-century palace, lush public spaces, fancy bars, a worthy splurge, RS%—use code "RICK."

Piazza Montecitorio 131, +39 06 695 001, www.hotelnazionale.it

$$$$ Albergo Santa Chiara Big, solid, all the hotel services, rooms are quiet and spacious, RS%—use code "RICK"; air-con, elevator.

Via di Santa Chiara 21, +39 06 687 2979, www.albergosantachiara.com

$$$$ Hotel Portoghesi Classic hotel, colorful rooms, peaceful, quiet, roof terrace, air-con, elevator.

Via dei Portoghesi 1, +39 06 686 4231, www.hotelportoghesiroma.it

PANTHEON NEIGHBORHOOD: NEAR CAMPO DE' FIORI

Winding lanes, fountains, markets, maximum Roman ambiance but pricey, near Largo Argentina bus and tram hub.

$$$$ Relais Teatro Argentina Old-Rome elegance with all the modern comforts, cozy and quiet, centrally located, air-con.

Via del Sudario 35, +39 06 9893 1617, www.relaisteatroargentina.com

$$$ Arch Rome Suites Tranquil palace on the site of the former Baths of Agrippa, family rooms, air-con, elevator.

Via dell'Arco della Ciambella 19, +39 06 4549 8947, www.archromesuites.it

$$$ Casa di Santa Brigida Lavish 20-room convent, beautiful public spaces, roof terrace, book well in advance, air-con, elevator.

Via di Monserrato 54, +39 06 6889 2596, www.brigidine.org

$$$ Hotel Smeraldo Reasonable deal in a good location, some rooms in an annex, air-con, elevator, roof terrace.

Via dei Chiavari 20, +39 06 687 5929, www.smeraldoroma.com

TRASTEVERE

Colorful and genuine, residential and bohemian neighborhood, served by trams #3 and #8 and buses #23 and #H.

$$$$ Residenza Arco dei Tolomei Six small, unique, antique-filled rooms, some with balconies, reserve well in advance, air-con.

Via dell'Arco de' Tolomei 27, +39 06 5832 0819, www.bbarcodeitolomei.com

$$$$ Hotel Santa Maria Small but well-equipped rooms circle a gravelly courtyard of orange trees, RS%, family rooms, air-con.

Vicolo del Piede 2, +39 06 589 4626, www.hotelsantamariatrastevere.it

$$$ Hotel San Francesco Big and modern yet welcoming, inviting roof terrace, email reservations preferred, air-con, elevator.

Via Jacopa de' Settesoli 7, +39 06 5830 0051, www.hotelsanfrancesco.net

$$$ Arco del Lauro B&B Six straightforward rooms around a quiet back courtyard, includes small breakfast at nearby café, air-con.

Via dell'Arco de' Tolomei 29, +39 346 244 3212, www.arcodellauro.it

SLEEPING

NEAR VATICAN CITY

Costs a little more, but in a relaxed, residential neighborhood handy to the Vatican (everything else is a long way away), near Cipro or Ottaviano Metro stops.

$$$$ Hotel dei Consoli Family-run, pleasantly located, rooftop terrace, RS%, air-con, elevator.
Via Varrone 2D, +39 06 6889 2972, www.hoteldeiconsoli.com

$$$$ Tmark Hotel Vaticano Facing the Vatican Museums, spacious rooms, modern comforts, air-con, elevator.
Viale Vaticano 99, +39 06 3974 5562, www.tmarkhotelvaticano.it

$$$$ Hearth Hotel A block from the Vatican wall; 22 small, efficient, and characterless rooms; RS%—use code "rick steves," air-con, elevator.
Via Santamaura 2, +39 06 3903 8383, www.hearthhotel.com

$$$ Hotel Museum Steps from the Vatican Museums, modest but comfortable rooms, family rooms, air-con, elevator.
Via Tunisi 8, +39 06 9727 6695, www.hotelmuseum.it

$$ Casa Valdese Church-run hotel, good value, renovated—but basic—rooms, roof terraces with views, family rooms, air-con, elevator.
Via Alessandro Farnese 18, +39 06 321 5362, www.casavaldeseroma.it

Eating

The Italians are masters of the art of fine eating. Lingering over a multicourse meal at an outdoor table watching a parade of passersby while you sip wine with loved ones...it's one of Rome's great pleasures.

I list a full range of eateries, from budget options for a quick bite to multicourse splurges with maximum ambience. They're located in neighborhoods handy to sightseeing, hotels, and atmosphere—see the maps on pages 193-196. Many of my listings offer outdoor seating, even in winter, thanks to patio heaters. I prefer mom-and-pop, personality-driven places with a local clientele. I appreciate both quality food and atmosphere, and my listings offer a reasonable balance of both.

I'm impressed by how small the price difference can be between a mediocre Roman restaurant and a fine one. If I had $100 for three meals in Rome, I'd spend $50 for one and $25 each for the other two, rather than $33 on all three.

Restaurant Code

Dollar signs reflect the cost of a typical main course.

$$$$	**Splurge:** Most main courses over €25
$$$	**Pricier:** €20-25
$$	**Moderate:** €15-20
$	**Budget:** Under €15

Pizza by the slice and other takeaway food is **$**; a basic trattoria or sit-down pizzeria is **$$**; a casual but more upscale restaurant is **$$$**; and a swanky splurge is **$$$$**.

When in Rome...

When in Rome, I eat on the Roman schedule. For breakfast, I eat at the hotel or grab a pastry and cappuccino at the neighborhood bar. Lunch—which traditionally was the biggest Italian meal of the day—is now more commonly a quick pasta or a takeout sandwich (*panino* or *tramezzino*), great for an atmospheric picnic. In the late afternoon, many Romans enjoy an after-work *aperitivo* and snack (*spuntino*). Dinner is the time for slowing down and savoring a restaurant meal.

Restaurants

Restaurants serve lunch 13:00-15:00 (and rarely open their doors before noon). Dinner is served to Romans from 20:00-22:00 and to tourists at 19:00 (quality restaurants rarely open any earlier).

While the word *ristorante* is self-explanatory, you'll also see other names for sit-down Italian restaurants. Trattoria and *osteria* imply a homey establishment, and pizzerias, *enotecas,* and *birrerias* specialize more in pizza, wine, and beer than full-course meals, but there are no hard-and-fast distinctions.

A full restaurant meal comes in courses: an antipasto, a plate of pasta, salad (either before or after the pasta course—your choice), the meat course, dessert, coffee, liqueurs, and so on. It can take hours, and the costs can add up quickly, so plan your strategy before sitting down to a restaurant meal.

For light eaters, there's nothing wrong with ordering a single dish as your meal—a plate of pasta, a pizza, an antipasto, or a salad. A good strategy for light-eating couples is to share a total of four dishes—e.g., one antipasto, one pasta, one meat course, and one dessert (or whatever combination appeals). Larger groups can share a variety of dishes from several courses, family style. Another good-value option common in Rome is self-serve buffets of cold and cooked *antipasti* (like a salad bar).

If you want a full meal at a predictable price, consider the *menù del giorno*—a fixed-price multicourse meal where you can choose from a list of menu items. It usually includes the service charge and can be a good value (avoid the cheaper *menù turistico*).

In Rome, only rude waiters rush you. For speedier service, be prepared with your next request whenever a waiter happens to grace your table. You'll have to ask for the bill—mime-scribble on your raised palm or ask: *"Il conto?"*

Quick Budget Meals

Rome offers many budget options for hungry travelers.

Italian "bars" are not taverns but cafés. These neighborhood hangouts serve coffee, sandwiches (grilled *panini* or cold *tramezzini*), minipizzas, premade salads, fresh-squeezed orange juice (*spremuta*), and drinks from the cooler.

Various cafeteria-style places (*tavola calda, rosticceria,* or just "cafeteria") dish out fast and cheap cooked meals to eat there or take out. You can buy pizza by the slice at little hole-in-the-wall places, sold by weight (100 grams for a small slice). A wine bar (*enoteca*) sells wine by the glass, but they also serve meat-and-cheese-type plates for the business crowd at lunch and happy hour. Trendy cocktail lounges offer free happy-hour buffets for the price of an (overpriced) drink—often a good value.

At any eating establishment (however humble), be aware that the price of your food and drink may be 20-40 percent more if you consume it while sitting at a table instead of standing at the bar. This two-tier price system will always be clearly posted. At many bars, the custom is to first pay the cashier for what you want, then hand the receipt to a barista who serves you.

A good budget option is to assemble a picnic and dine with Rome as your backdrop. Buy ingredients for your picnic at one of Rome's open-air produce markets (mornings only), an *alimentari* (corner grocery store), a *rosticcerie,* or a *supermercato,* such as Conad or Co-op. Note that Rome discourages people from picnicking or drinking at historic monuments (such as at the Pantheon) in the old center. Violators can

be fined. You'll be OK if you eat *with* a view rather than *in* the view and remain discreet. Also, when buying produce, it's customary to let the merchant pick it out. If something is a mystery, ask for a small taste— *"un assaggio, per favore."*

Roman Cuisine

Rome has a few specialties: *spaghetti alla carbonara* (in egg-pancetta sauce), *gnocchi alla romana* (dumplings), *carciofi alla giudia* (fried artichokes), *saltimbocca alla romana* (veal), pecorino romano cheese (from ewe's milk), and *trippa alla romana* (tripe—intestines—as good as it sounds).

No meal in Italy is complete without wine. Even the basic house wine (*vino da tavola* or *vino della casa*) is a good choice. The region around Rome produces Frascati (an inexpensive dry white) and Torre Ercolana (an expensive, aged, dense red). You'll also find lots of Chiantis and Montepulcianos from Tuscany (for an upgrade, pay more for a Brunello di Montalcino); well-aged Barbaresco and Barolo from Piedmont; and crisp white Orvieto Classico.

Popular before-dinner *aperitivi* are Campari and Cynar. After-dinner liqueurs include *amaro* (various brands) and anise-flavored Sambuca.

Italian coffee is excellent. Even basic bars serve espresso, *macchiatos*, and cappuccinos. In the summer, Romans like a sugared iced coffee called *caffè freddo*. Streetside vendors sell *grattachecca* (grah-tah-KEK-kah): shaved ice with fruit syrup.

For dessert, try *tartufo*—a rich dark-chocolate gelato ball. Or pick up a cup or cone of gelato at a *gelateria,* and join the rest of Rome, strolling the streets and enjoying a slice of edible art.

For the latest on the Roman food scene, see KatieParla.com. For food-themed guided walks, see EatingEurope.com. For evening wine-tasting classes, see VinoRoma.com.

ANCIENT ROME: MONTI NEIGHBORHOOD

Characteristic, trendy neighborhood, action centers on Piazza della Madonna dei Monti (see map, page 193).

1 **$$ Barzilai Bistrot** Wine bar with kitchen, family-run, fun menu ranging from pastas to burgers, no reservations (daily 9:00-24:00, Sun until 18:00).
Via Panisperna 44, +39 06 487 4979

2 **$$ Taverna Romana** Small, simple, a bit chaotic, family-run, *cacio e pepe* (cheese-and-pepper pasta) is a favorite, book ahead at busy times (daily 12:30-14:45 & 19:00-22:45).
Via della Madonna dei Monti 79, +39 06 474 5325, www.monti79.it

3 **$$$ Taverna dei Fori Imperiali** Typical Roman cuisine, snug interior, energetic, reserve for dinner (Wed-Mon 12:30-15:00 & 19:30-22:30, closed Tue).
Via della Madonna dei Monti 9, +39 06 679 8643, www.latavernadeiforiimperiali.com

4 **$$ Alle Carrette Pizzeria** Simple, rustic, family-friendly, 200 yards from Forum, cheap and fast (daily 12:00-15:30 & 19:00-24:00).
Vicolo delle Carrette 14, +39 06 679 2770

5 **$$ Trattoria Valentino** Classic, specializes in *scamorza* (grilled cheese with various toppings), daily pasta specials (Mon-Sat 13:00-14:45 & 19:30-23:00, closed Sun).
Via del Boschetto 37, +39 06 488 0643

6 **$ Antico Forno ai Serpenti** Hip bakery with a few tables, panini, lasagna, good bread, breakfasts, order at the counter (daily 7:00-22:00).
Via dei Serpenti 122, +39 06 4542 7920

7 **$$ Enoteca Cavour 313** Quality wine bar, salads, *affettati* (cold cuts) and cheese, mellow ambience (Mon-Sat 12:30-14:45 & 18:00-23:30, closed Sun).
Via Cavour 313, +39 06 678 5496

ANCIENT ROME: NEAR THE COLOSSEUM

Residential zone just up the street from Colosseum with a variety of restaurants (see map, page 193).

8 **$ Trattoria Luzzi** Well worn, simple food, high energy, good prices, big portions, reserve ahead (Thu-Tue 12:00-24:00, closed Wed).
Via Celimontana 1, +39 06 709 6332

9 **$$ Ristorante Pizzeria Naumachia** A solid bet, upscale, tasty pastas and pizza (daily 11:00-23:00).
Via Celimontana 7, +39 06 700 2764

10 **$$ Li Rioni** Open only for dinner, terrace out front, crispy-crust Roman-style pizzas (Wed-Mon 19:30-24:00, closed Tue).
Via dei SS. Quattro 24, +39 06 7045 0605

EATING

NEAR TERMINI STATION

Best dining options are about a 10-minute walk from the station, close to recommended accommodations (see map, page 193).

⑪ **$$$ Target Restaurant** Sleek and dressy ambience, food good but pricey, reservations smart (daily 12:00-15:30 & 19:00-24:00, closed Sun at lunch).
Via Torino 33, +39 06 474 0066, www.targetrestaurant.it

⑫ **$$ Café Pasticceria Dagnino** Time-warp eatery, known for its pastry section and Sicilian treats, reasonably priced, good seating (daily 7:00-23:00).
Galleria Esedra, enter at Via Torino 95, +39 06 481 8660

⑬ **$ Caffè Torino Tavola Calda** Quick, cheap lunch, fresh dishes for a fine price (Mon-Fri 6:00-16:00, closed Sat-Sun).
Via Torino 40, +39 06 487 0000

⑭ **$ Il Forno degli Amici** Handy location, salads sold by weight, pizza by the slice, sandwiches, bakery items (Mon-Sat until 21:00, closed Sun).
Via Firenze 51

⑮ **$$$ Ristorante la Pentolaccia** Upscale and romantic, tourist-friendly, tight seating, traditional Roman cooking, daily specials, reservations smart (daily 12:00-15:00 & 18:00-23:00).
Via Flavia 38, +39 06 483 477, www.lapentolaccia-restaurant.it

⑯ **$$$ La Bottega Ristorante** Family-run, bright, contemporary, easygoing, Roman and Mediterranean cuisine, good wine by the glass (nightly from 17:00).
Via Flavia 46, +39 06 487 0391

⑰ **$ Punturi** High-end *rosticceria,* dishes sold by weight, fast-food-type seating (Mon-Sat 8:30-20:30, closed Sun).
Via Flavia 46

⑱ **$$$ I Colori del Vino Enoteca** Classy wine bar, creative menu, great list of fine wines by the glass, also good for dessert wine (Mon-Sat 12:00-15:00 & 18:00-23:00, closed Sun).
Via Aureliana 15 at corner of Via Flavia, +39 06 474 1745

⑲ **$$$ Hostaria Romana** Busy bistro, glassed-in terrace upstairs, noisy cellar, traditional Roman dishes, reservations smart (Mon-Sat 12:30-15:00 & 19:15-23:00, closed Sun and Aug).
Via del Boccaccio 1, +39 06 474 5284, www.hostariaromana.it

PANTHEON NEIGHBORHOOD: NEAR PIAZZA NAVONA

Square with amazing array of restaurants—head west for more authentic eateries (see map, page 194).

⑳ $$ Vivi Bistrot In the Museum of Rome, cheery and modern restaurant with salads, pastas, burger plates (Tue-Sun 10:00-24:00, closed Mon).
Piazza Navona 2, +39 06 683 3779

㉑ $$ Cul de Sac Trattoria filled with regulars, wide-ranging menu from pasta to homemade pâté, good wines by the glass, fine outdoor seating, no reservations (daily 12:00-23:00).
Piazza Pasquino 73, +39 06 6880 1094

㉒ $$ L'Insalata Ricca Popular local chain, filling salads and pasta (daily 12:00-24:00).
Largo dei Chiavari 85, +39 06 6880 3656

㉓ $$$ Ristorante Pizzeria "da Francesco" Bustling and authentic, reservations required for dinner, indoor/outdoor seating, daily specials (daily 12:00-16:00 & 19:00-24:00).
Piazza del Fico 29, +39 06 686 4009, www.dafrancesco.it

㉔ $ Pizzeria da Baffetto Famous and generally comes with a line, great pizza, tight tables (daily 12:00-15:30 & 18:00-late).
Via del Governo Vecchio 114, +39 06 686 1617

㉕ $$ Chiostro del Bramante Museum café, light lunches, unique setting, refined and elegant, fine for predinner drink (daily 10:00-20:00, meals served 12:00-15:00).
Arco della Pace 5, +39 06 6880 9035

PANTHEON NEIGHBORHOOD: NEAR THE PANTHEON

Walk a few blocks away from the Pantheon and Trevi Fountain to find these better alternatives (see map, page 194).

㉖ $$$ Origano Modern bistro and café, well priced, traditional Roman specialties (daily 12:00-24:00).
Via di Sant'Andrea delle Fratte 25, +39 06 6992 0907

㉗ $$ L'Antica Birreria Peroni Hearty mugs of the local Peroni beer, beer-hall food and Italian classics, a hit with Romans (Mon-Sat 12:00-24:00, closed Sun).
Via di San Marcello 19, +39 06 679 5310

㉘ $$$ Enoteca Corsi Family-run, traditional cuisine, daily specials, friendly staff (Mon-Sat 12:00-15:30, Wed-Fri also 19:15-22:30, closed Sun).
Via del Gesù 87, +39 06 679 0821

29 **$$ Da Gino al Parlamento** Favorite since 1963, traditional Roman cuisine, four seatings: 13:00, 14:30, 20:00, and 22:00; reserve ahead (closed Sun).

Vicolo Rosini 4, +39 06 687 3434, www.ristoranteparlamento.roma.it

30 **$$$ Ristorante la Campana** Appreciated by well-dressed locals, typical Roman dishes, daily specials, inside seating (Tue-Sun 12:30-15:00 & 19:30-23:00, closed Mon).

Vicolo della Campana 18, +39 06 687 5273, www.ristorantelacampana.com

31 **$$$ Osteria delle Coppelle** Trendy place, serves traditional dishes to a local crowd, rustic interior and jumbled exterior seating (daily 12:30-15:30 & 19:00-late).

Piazza delle Coppelle 54, +39 06 4550 2826

32 **$$$ Ginger** Modern, spacious and bright interior, menu is healthy, organic, and a bit pricey (daily 8:00-23:00).

Piazza di S. Eustachio 54, +39 06 6830 8559

33 **$$ Miscellanea** Sandwiches, pizza-like bruschetta, hearty salads, pasta, a good value for a cheap and filling dinner (daily 9:00-24:00).

Via della Palombella 37, +39 06 6813 5318

NEAR THE SPANISH STEPS
Upscale restaurants in chic neighborhood (see map, page 194).

34 **$$$$ Ristorante il Gabriello** Inviting and small, family-run, fresh organic products, reservations smart, dress respectfully (dinner only, Mon-Sat 19:00-23:00, closed Sun).

Via Vittoria 51, +39 06 6994 0810, www.ilgabriello.com

35 **$$$ Ginger** Bright, stylish with a pinch of posh and pretense; sister location next to the Pantheon, described above (daily 8:00-23:00).

Via Borgognona 43, +39 06 9603 6390

36 **$$$ Caffè Vitti** On traffic-free square, good salads and pizza, cocktails come with munchies (daily 6:30-24:00).

Piazza San Lorenzo in Lucina 33, +39 06 687 6304

PANTHEON NEIGHBORHOOD: NEAR CAMPO DE' FIORI

Lively square lined with popular bars, pizzerias, and small restaurants (see map, page 195).

37 **$$ Enoteca L'Angolo Divino** Inviting wine bar, run by sommelier; meats, cheeses, and pastas, tiny tables, memorable (daily 17:00-24:00 plus Tue-Sat 11:00-14:00).
Via dei Balestrari 12, +39 06 686 4413

38 **$ Antico Forno Roscioli** Attractive upscale bakery, a few stools, tempting array of breads, pizzas, and pastries (Mon-Sat 7:30-20:00 Sun 8:30-18:00).
Via dei Chiavari 34

39 **$ Filetti di Baccalà** Cheap and basic greasy spoon, nostalgic regulars at wooden tables, indoor/outdoor seating (Mon-Sat 17:00-23:00, closed Sun).
Largo dei Librari 88, +39 06 686 4018

40 **$$ Open Baladin** Busy, modern, spacious brewpub with burgers, salads, and freshly cooked potato chips, pricey (Mon-Fri 12:00-15:00 & 18:00-late, Sat-Sun 12:00-late).
Via degli Specchi 5, +39 06 683 8989

TRASTEVERE

A favorite dining neighborhood—more rustic than the downtown zone, eateries with sincerity and charm (see map, page 195).

41 **$$$$ Taverna Trilussa** Family-run, quality without pretense, award-winning *pasta amatriciana,* hedged-in terrace, reservations smart (dinner only, Mon-Sat from 19:30, closed Sun).
Via del Politeama 23, +39 06 581 8918, www.tavernatrilussa.it

42 **$$$ Dar Sor Olimpio al Drago** Romantic dining room, friendly staff, enticing menu—both typical Roman and modern Italian (Mon-Fri 18:00-23:00, Sat-Sun 12:30-16:00 & 18:30-23:00).
Piazza del Drago 2, +39 339 885 7574

43 **$$ Trattoria de Gli Amici** Employs people with developmental disabilities, delightful meals, charming atmosphere, traditional Roman cuisine (daily 12:00-23:00).
Piazza Sant'Egidio 6, +39 06 580 6033

44 **$$ La Prosciutteria Cantina dei Papi** Cozy, friendly; wine, cheese, and meats of Lazio and Tuscany; order at the counter (daily 12:00-24:00).
Via della Scala 71, +39 06 6456 2839

EATING

45 **$$ Pizzeria "Ai Marmi"** Tight tables, classic Roman scene; famously good, thin, and crispy pizza; long line starting at 20:00, cash only (Thu-Tue 18:30 until very late, closed Wed).

Viale di Trastevere 53, +39 06 580 0919

46 **$$ Pizzeria Dar Poeta,** Wood-fired pizzas and calzones in a back alley, pizzas are easily splittable, cramped interior or lively tables outside, reservations smart (daily 12:00-24:00; call to reserve, arrive before 19:00).

Vicolo del Bologna 45, +39 06 588 0516

NEAR VATICAN CITY

A stone's throw from the Vatican, mostly fast and cheap (see map, page 196).

47 **$$ Il Colibrì** Family-run, noisy streetside seating, quiet interior (daily 10:30-15:30 & 19:00-24:00).

Via Famagosta 69, +39 06 3751 4767

48 **$ Be.Re.** Trendy, variety of microbrews, doughy "pizza pockets" with toasted crusts (daily 10:00-late).

Via Vespasiano 2, +39 06 9442 1854

49 **$ L'Insalata Ricca** Popular chain, serves hearty salads and pastas (daily 12:00-23:30).

Piazza Risorgimento 5, +39 06 3973 0387

50 **$ Duecento Gradi** Fresh and creative sandwiches, expensive by Roman standards, eat sitting down or take it away (daily 11:00-24:00).

Piazza Risorgimento 3, +39 06 3975 4239

51 **$$ Tre Pupazzi** Traditional Roman cuisine—lamb, beef shanks, *saltimbocca*, fettucine with truffles; occasional Portuguese specialties (Mon-Sat 12:00-15:00 & 19:00-23:00, closed Sun).

Borgo Pio 183, +39 06 6880 3220)

52 **$ Vecchio Borgo** Pasta, pizza by weight, and veggies to go or to eat at simple tables (daily 9:30-22:30).

Borgo Pio 27a

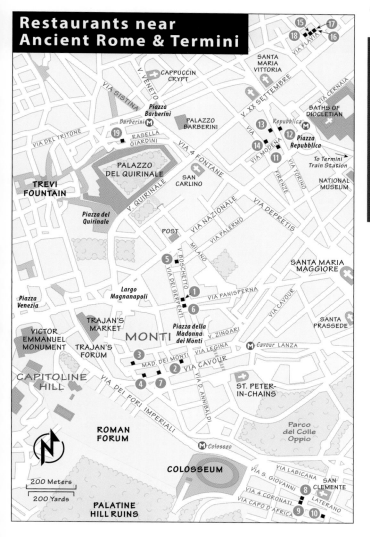

Restaurants near Ancient Rome & Termini

200 Meters
200 Yards

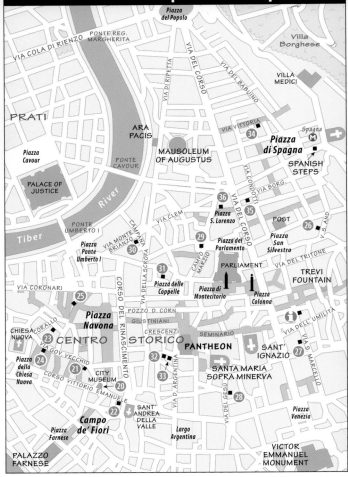

Restaurants near the Pantheon & Spanish Steps

Restaurants near Campo de'Fiori & in Trastevere

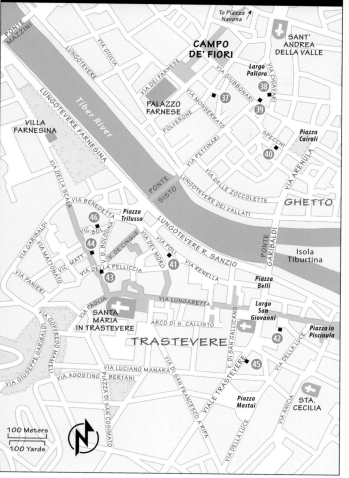

To Piazza Navona

CAMPO DE'FIORI

SANT' ANDREA DELLA VALLE

Largo Pallaro

PONTE MAZZINI

VIA GIULIA

LUNGOTEVERE

VIA DEI FARNESE

VIA GIUBBONARI

VIA CHIAVARI

37

38

PALAZZO FARNESE

VIA MONSERRATO

39

POLVERONE

Piazza Cairoli

VILLA FARNESINA

Tiber River

LUNGOTEVERE FARNESINA

VIA DELLA SCALA

VIA PETTINARI

SPECCHI

40

VIA ARENULA

VIA DELLE ZOCCOLETTE

PONTE SISTO

LUNGOTEVERE DEI VALLATI

GHETTO

VIA BENEDETTA

Piazza Trilussa

46

PONTE GARIBALDI

LUNGOTEVERE R. SANZIO

Isola Tiburtina

VIA GARIBALDI

VIA MATTONATO

VIG. BOLOGNA

44

V. D. BOLOGNA

V. DE CINQUE

VIA DEL MORO

VIA POLI

VIA RENELLA

VIA PANIERI

VIA DELLA PELLICCIA

41

43

Piazza Belli

VIA PAGLIA

VIA LUNGARETTA

Largo San Giovanni

SANTA MARIA IN TRASTEVERE

ARCO DI S. CALLISTO

V. D. SAN GALLICANO

Piazza in Piscinula

VIA GOFFREDO GARIBALDI

TRASTEVERE

42

VIA DELLA LUCE

VIA GIUSEPPE GARIBALDI

VIA LUCIANO MANARA

VIALE TRASTEVERE

45

VIA AGOSTINO BERTANI

PIAZZA DI SAN COSIMATO

VIA DI SAN FRANCESCO A RIPA

Piazza Mastai

VIA ANICIA

STA. CECILIA

VIA DELLA LUCE

100 Meters

100 Yards

Restaurants near Vatican City

Piazzale
degli
Eroi

VIA ANDREA DORIA

VIA FAMAGOSTA

VIALE GIULIO CESARE

MERCATO
TRIONFALE

47

Ⓜ Ottaviano

VIA CARACCIOLO

Piazza
S. Maria
Grazie

Ⓜ Cipro

VIA CANDIA

VIA SEB. VENIERO

VIALE VATICANO

VIA COLA DI RIENZO

48

49

Piazza
Risorgimento

50

VIA CRESCENZIO

VATICAN
MUSEUMS

BORGO ANGELICO

VATICAN
CITY

BORGO VITTORIO

BORGO PIO

51

52

ST. PETER'S

St. Peter's
Square

VIA CONCILIAZIONE

200 Meters

200 Yards

VIA PORTA
CAVALLEGGERI

To
San Pietro
Station

TUNNEL

PONTE
AMEDEO

Tiber

Practicalities

Helpful Hints 198
Arrival in Rome 200
Getting Around Rome 202
Money. 206
Staying Connected. 207
Resources from Rick Steves 208
Packing Checklist 209
Italian Survival Phrases 211

Travel Tips

Travel Advisories: Before traveling, check updated health and safety conditions, including restrictions for your destination, on the travel pages of the US State Department (www.travel.state.gov) and Centers for Disease Control and Prevention (www.cdc.gov/travel).

Tourist information: Rome has small city-run tourist information offices scattered around town that sell sightseeing passes and maps (typically open daily 9:00-19:00, shorter hours off-season possible, www.turismoroma.it). The largest TIs are at both airports (Fiumicino Terminal 3 and Ciampino) and at Termini train station (at the far end of the concourse that runs along track 24—either loop around outside or cut through the department store). For practical information, it's more helpful to visit www.060608.it or utilize Rome's call center (+39 06 0608, answered daily 9:00-19:00, press 2 for English).

Sightseeing Tips: Despite the huge crowds inundating Rome, you'll only find lines a problem at St. Peter's Basilica (go early or late to minimize) and Vatican Museums (easy to avoid by booking in advance online). Tickets for the Colosseum, the Roman Forum, and Palatine Hill must be reserved in advance (no on-site sales), and for the Colosseum, you must book a specific entrance time. The Borghese Gallery also requires a timed-entry ticket purchased in advance. The Pantheon often has a long line that moves fast, but on weekends you'll likely need to book ahead to enter. For any sight, be sure that you're booking on the official website (listed in this book), rather than a third-party scalper site.

Time Zones: Italy is six/nine hours ahead of the East/West Coasts of the US. For a handy time converter, use the world clock app on your phone or download one (see www.timeanddate.com).

Business Hours: Stores are often closed on Sundays, summer Saturday afternoons, and winter Monday mornings. Banking hours are generally Monday through Friday 8:30 to 13:30 and 15:30 to 16:30, but can vary wildly.

Watt's Up: Europe's electrical system is 220 volts, instead of North America's 110 volts. Most electronics (laptops, phones, cameras) and appliances (newer hair dryers, CPAP machines) convert automatically, so you won't need a converter, but you will need an adapter plug with two round prongs, sold inexpensively at travel stores in the US.

Helpful Websites

Rome Tourist Information: TurismoRoma.it
Italian Tourist Information: Italia.it
Passports and Red Tape: Travel.state.gov
Cheap Flights: Kayak.com (for international flights), SkyScanner.com (for flights within Europe)
Airplane Carry-on Restrictions: TSA.gov
The Vatican: Vatican.va and MuseiVaticani.va
Rome Entertainment and Current Events: WantedinRome.com
European Train Schedules: Bahn.com
General Travel Tips: RickSteves.com (train travel, rail passes, car rental, travel insurance, packing lists, and much more—plus updates to this book)

Safety and Emergencies

Emergency and Medical Help: For any emergency service—ambulance, police, or fire—call **112** from a mobile phone or landline. If you get sick, do as the locals do and go to a pharmacist for advice. Or ask at your hotel for help—they'll know the nearest medical and emergency services.

Theft or Loss: While violent crime is rare in the city center, petty theft is rampant. With sweet-talking con artists meeting you at the station, well-dressed pickpockets on buses, and fast-fingered moms with babies at the ancient sites, Rome is a gauntlet of rip-offs: Wear your money belt.

To replace a **passport,** you'll need to go in person to an embassy. If your **credit and debit cards** disappear, cancel and replace them, and report the loss immediately (with a mobile phone, call these 24-hour US numbers: Visa—+1 303 967 1096, MasterCard—+1 636 722 7111, and American Express—+1 336 393 1111). For more information, see RickSteves.com/help.

To report lost or stolen items, file a police report (at Termini station, with *polizia* at track 11 or with carabinieri at track 20; offices are also at Piazza Venezia and at the corner of Via Nazionale and Via Genova).

Around Town

Bookstores: Borri Books, a large chain store at Termini station, sells English-language books (open daily). The **Anglo-American Bookshop** has great art and history sections (closed Sun, a few blocks south of Spanish Steps at Via della Vite 102). In Trastevere, the **Almost Corner Bookshop** stocks an extensive Italian-interest section (Via del Moro 45), and the **Open Door Bookshop** carries the only used books in English in town (Via della Lungaretta 23).

Laundry: Coin launderettes are common in Rome. Your hotelier can direct you to the closest one (or search on Google Maps for "laundry").

Pharmacies: Bigger pharmacies that stay open late cluster around Termini station: There's one inside the station itself (along northeast side, enter from Via Marsala, +39 06 474 5421); another south of the station, at the corner of Via Cavour (Piazza dei Cinquecento 51); and **Farmacia Piram** (Via Nazionale 228, +39 06 488 4437).

ARRIVAL IN ROME

Fiumicino (Leonardo da Vinci) Airport

Rome's main airport has ATMs, banks, shops, bars, and a tourist information office (in Terminal 3, daily 9:00-17:30). For airport information, visit www.adr.it (code: FCO).

To get between the airport and downtown Rome, you have several options:

"Leonardo Express" Train: A direct train connects the airport and Rome's central Termini train station in 32 minutes for €14. Departures are twice hourly from roughly 6:00 to 23:00. From the airport's arrival gate, follow signs with a train icon or *Stazione/Railway Station.* Buy your ticket from a Trenitalia machine, the ticket office (*biglietteria*), or a newsstand; then validate it in a green-and-gray machine near the track. You can also use the Trenitalia app on your smartphone. Make sure the train you board is going to the central "Roma Termini" station, as trains from the airport serve other destinations, too.

Going from Termini to the airport, trains depart from track 23 or 24. Buy the €14 ticket at the platform from self-service machines or a newsstand.

Taxi: A taxi between Fiumicino and any destination in downtown Rome takes 45 minutes in normal traffic and costs an official fixed rate of €50 for up to four people with bags. To get this fare, catch your taxi at the airport's taxi stand, and only use an official Rome city cab (white with a *taxi* sign on the roof and a maroon *Roma Capitale* logo on the door). Avoid unmarked, unmetered taxis or other cab companies; these guys will try to tempt you away from the taxi-stand lineup by offering an immediate (rip-off) ride. When you're departing Rome, your hotel can arrange a taxi to the airport at any hour.

Shuttle Bus: Shared shuttle-van services can be economical for one or two people. Consider **Rome Airport Shuttle** (€25 for one person, extra people-€6 each, by reservation only, +39 06 4201 4507 or +39 06 4201 3469, www.airportshuttle.it).

Ciampino Airport: Rome's smaller airport (code: CIA, www.adr.it) handles charter flights and some budget airlines (including most Ryanair flights). To get to downtown Rome, Terravision (www.terravision.eu), SIT (www.sitbusshuttle.com), and Schiaffini (www.romeairportbus.com) buses connect Ciampino and Termini (about €5, 2/hour, 45 minutes). Rome Airport Shuttle (listed above) also offers service. A taxi should cost about €31.

Termini Train Station

Of Rome's four main train stations, by far the most important is the centrally located Termini Station, which has connections to the airport. Termini is a buffet of tourist services: information desks, cheap eateries, a large Sapori & Dintori supermarket (downstairs), late-hours banks, a good-sized bookstore, and 24-hour thievery—avoid anybody selling anything unless they're in a legitimate shop.

Termini is a major transportation hub. The city's two Metro lines (A and B) intersect at Termini Metro station (downstairs). City buses, taxis, and the hop-on, hop-off bus tours leave from the front of the station.

Exiting near track 24, about 100 yards down the street you'll find a tourist information office (TI, daily 9:30-19:00). The station also has a car rental desk and baggage storage.

To buy train tickets or make reservations, avoid Termini's long lines by buying online (www.trenitalia.com), from the station's ticket machines, from an uncrowded travel agency near your Rome hotel, or use the Trenitalia smartphone app. There is also a private train company called Italo (www.italotreno.it) that runs fast trains from Termini to major destinations across Italy.

Other Arrival Points

Tiburtina Station: Some high-speed trains and many regional buses (e.g., from Siena or Sorrento) arrive here in the city's northeast corner (Metro: Tiburtina).

Arrival by Car: Don't drive in traffic-choked Rome. If you must arrive by car, get parking advice from your hotel. Or take the Settebagni exit, follow Centro signs, and park at the Villa Borghese underground garage (€20/day, Viale del Galoppatoio 33, Metro: Spagna, www.sabait.it).

By Cruise Ship: Cruise ships dock at Civitavecchia (45 miles northwest of Rome), a 1.5-hour drive or 40-80-minute train ride to Rome. The cheapest way to get to Rome is by train: Ride the free shuttle bus from your ship to the port's transit center (Largo della Pace), then take a city bus (€2, 6/hour) to the Civitavecchia train station where you can catch a train to Rome (hourly departures). Several private companies offer cheap bus transfers from the transit hub to Rome or Rome's airports (try Civita Tours, +39 346 217 7803, www.civitatours.com). A taxi to central Rome (they'll be waiting at the dock, eager to overcharge you) should cost around €150-200 one-way.

GETTING AROUND ROME

I've grouped your sightseeing into walkable neighborhoods. To connect sights beyond walking distance, you can ride the Metro or a city bus, or take a taxi. As Rome is a great taxi town (most rides cost €8-12), especially for couples and families, I'd rely more on taxis than public transit.

Tickets

All public transportation uses the same ticket. It costs €1.50 and is valid for one Metro ride—including transfers underground—plus unlimited city buses and trams during a 100-minute period. Passes good on buses and the Metro are sold in increments of 24 hours (€7), 48 hours (€12.50), 72 hours (€18), and so on.

You can purchase tickets and passes from machines at Metro stations and a few major bus stops, and from some newsstands and tobacco shops (*tabacchi,* marked by a black-and-white *T* sign). Tickets are not sold on board. It's smart to stock up on tickets early.

By Metro

The Roman subway system (Metropolitana, or "Metro") is simple, clean, cheap, and fast. The two lines you need to know—A and B—intersect at Termini station. Validate your ticket by sticking it in the Metro turnstile (magnetic strip-side up, arrow-side first). To get through a Metro turnstile with a transit pass, tap the card against the turnstile's sensor.

By Bus

The Metro is handy, but it won't get you everywhere—you often have to take the bus (or tram). Bus routes are listed at each stop. Route and system maps aren't posted, but with some knowledge of major stops, you can wing it without one. Rome's few tram lines function identically to buses.

Buses—especially the touristy #40 and #64—are havens for thieves and pickpockets. If one bus is packed, there's likely a second one on its tail with far fewer crowds and thieves. Or read the signs posted at stops to see if a different, less crowded bus route can get you to or near your destination.

On buses, tickets must be inserted in the yellow box with the digital readout (magnetic-strip-side down, arrow-side first; be sure to retrieve your ticket after it's spit out). You don't need to validate a ticket or pass on the bus if you've already validated it elsewhere. Bus etiquette (not always followed) is to board at the front or rear doors and exit at the middle.

By Taxi and Uber

I use taxis in Rome more often than in other cities. Three or four companions with more money than time should taxi almost everywhere. Taxis start at €3, then charge about €1.50 per kilometer (surcharges: €1.50 on Sun, €3.50 for nighttime hours of 22:00-6:00, one regular suitcase or bag rides free, tip by rounding up—€1 or so). Sample fares: Termini area to Vatican—€15; Termini area to Colosseum—€8; Termini area to the Borghese Gallery—€10; Colosseum to Trastevere—€12 (or look up your route at www.worldtaximeter.com).

You can always hail a cab on the street. But Romans generally walk to the nearest taxi stand (*fermata dei taxi,* many are marked on this book's maps) or have your hotel or restaurant call a taxi for you. The meter starts when the call is received. To call a cab on your own, dial +39 06 3570, +39 06 4994, or +39 06 6645, or use the official city taxi

Rome's Metro

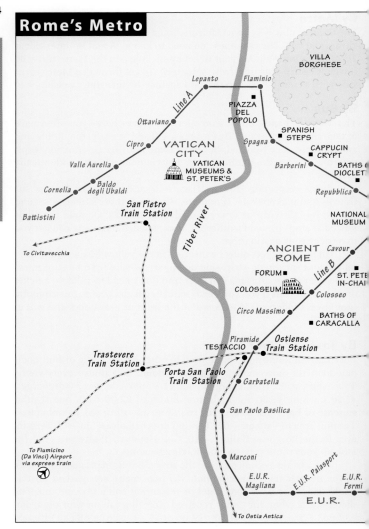

VILLA BORGHESE

Lepanto

Flaminio

Line A

PIAZZA DEL POPOLO

Ottaviano

SPANISH STEPS

Cipro

VATICAN CITY

Spagna

CAPPUCIN CRYPT

Valle Aurelia

VATICAN MUSEUMS & ST. PETER'S

Barberini

BATHS OF DIOCLET

Cornelia

Baldo degli Ubaldi

Repubblica

Battistini

San Pietro Train Station

NATIONAL MUSEUM

To Civitavecchia

Tiber River

ANCIENT ROME

Cavour

FORUM

Line B

ST. PETE IN-CHAI

COLOSSEUM

Colosseo

Circo Massimo

BATHS OF CARACALLA

Piramide

Ostiense Train Station

TESTACCIO

Trastevere Train Station

Porta San Paolo Train Station

Garbatella

San Paolo Basilica

To Fiumicino (Da Vinci) Airport via express train

Marconi

E.U.R. Magliana

E.U.R. Palasport

E.U.R. Fermi

E.U.R.

To Ostia Antica

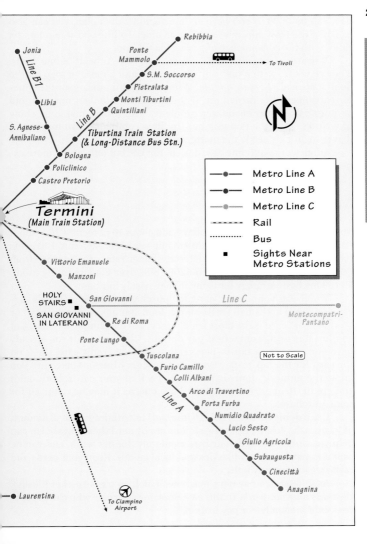

line, +39 06 0609. If you have an international data plan, you can also use the **Free Now** app, which orders an official white taxi at regular taxi rates, with the convenience of paying via the app.

Beware of corrupt taxis. First, only use official Rome taxis. They're white, with a taxi sign on the roof and a maroon logo on the door that reads *Roma Capitale*. When you get in, make sure the meter (*tassametro*) is turned on. If the meter isn't on, get out and find another cab. If you encounter problems with a taxi, making a show of writing down the taxi number (to file a complaint) can motivate a driver to quickly settle the matter.

Uber works in Rome as it does in the US, but only at the more expensive Uber Black level.

MONEY

To convert prices in euros to dollars, add about 10 percent: €20 = about $22, €50 = about $55. Like the dollar, one euro is broken into 100 cents (check www.oanda.com for the latest exchange rates). Coins range from €0.01 to €2, and bills from €5 to €200 (bills over €50 are rarely used). Here's my basic strategy for using money wisely in Rome.

You'll use your credit card for purchases both big (hotels, advance tickets) and small (little shops, food stands). A "tap-to-pay" or "contactless" card is the most widely accepted and simplest to use. Get comfortable using contactless pay options. Check to see if you already have—or can get—a tap-to-pay version of your credit card (look on the card for the tap-to-pay symbol—four curvy lines). Make sure you know the numeric, four-digit PIN for each of your cards, both debit and credit. Request it if you don't have one, as it may be required for some purchases.

Use a **debit card** at ATMs (*bancomat*) to withdraw a small amount of local cash. While most transactions are by card these days, cash can help you out of a jam if your card randomly doesn't work, and can be useful to pay for things like tips and local guides. Keep your cards and cash safe in a **money belt.**

At self-service payment machines (such as transit-ticket kiosks), US cards may not work. In this case, look for a cashier who can process your card manually—or pay in cash.

Tipping

Tipping in Italy isn't as automatic and generous as it is in the US.

Restaurants: In Italy, a service charge (*servizio*) is usually built into your check (look at the bill carefully). If it is included, there's no need to leave an extra tip. If it's not included, it's common to leave about €1 per person (a bit more at finer restaurants) or to round up the bill.

Taxis: For a typical ride, round up your fare a bit (for instance, if the fare is €4.50, pay €5).

Services: In general, if someone in the tourism or service industry does a super job for you, a small tip of a euro or two is appropriate...but not required.

STAYING CONNECTED

Making International Calls

From a Mobile Phone: Phone numbers in this book are presented exactly as you would dial them from a US mobile phone. For international access, press and hold 0 (zero) to get a + sign, then dial the country code (39 for Italy) and phone number.

From a US Landline to Europe: Replace + with 011 (US/Canada access code), then dial the country code (39 for Italy) and phone number.

From a European Landline to the US or Europe: Replace + with 00 (Europe access code), then dial the country code (39 for Italy, 1 for the US) and phone number. For more phoning help, check out HowToCallAbroad.com.

Using Your Phone in Europe

Sign up for an international plan. To stay connected at a lower cost, sign up for an international service plan through your carrier. Most providers offer a simple bundle that includes calling, messaging, and data.

Use free Wi-Fi whenever possible. Unless you have an unlimited-data plan, save most of your online tasks for Wi-Fi. Most accommodations in Europe offer free Wi-Fi, and many cafés offer hotspots for customers. You may also find Wi-Fi at TIs, city squares, major museums, public-transit hubs, airports, and aboard trains and buses.

Minimize use of your cellular network. Even with an international data plan, wait until you're on Wi-Fi to Skype or FaceTime, download apps, stream videos, or do other megabyte-greedy tasks. Using a navigation app such as Google Maps over a cellular network can require lots of data, so download maps when you're on Wi-Fi, then use the app offline.

Use Wi-Fi calling and messaging apps. Skype, WhatsApp, FaceTime, and Google Meet are great for making free or low-cost calls or sending texts over Wi-Fi worldwide.

RESOURCES FROM RICK STEVES

Begin your trip at RickSteves.com: This book is just one of many in my series on European travel. I also produce a public television series, *Rick Steves' Europe,* and a public radio show, *Travel with Rick Steves.* My mobile-friendly website is *the* place to explore Europe in preparation for your trip. You'll find thousands of fun articles, videos, and radio interviews; a wealth of money-saving tips; travel news dispatches; a video library of travel talks; my travel blog; our latest guidebook updates (RickSteves.com/update); and the free Rick Steves Audio Europe app with audio tours of Europe's top sights. You can also follow me on Facebook, Instagram, and Twitter.

Packing Checklist

Clothing

- ❏ 5 shirts: long- & short-sleeve
- ❏ 2 pairs pants (or skirts/capris)
- ❏ 1 pair shorts
- ❏ 5 pairs underwear & socks
- ❏ 1 pair walking shoes
- ❏ Sweater or warm layer
- ❏ Rainproof jacket with hood
- ❏ Tie, scarf, belt, and/or hat
- ❏ Swimsuit
- ❏ Sleepwear/loungewear

Money

- ❏ Debit card(s)
- ❏ Credit card(s)
- ❏ Hard cash (US $100-200)
- ❏ Money belt

Documents

- ❏ Passport
- ❏ Other required ID: Vaccine card/Covid test, entry visa, etc.
- ❏ Driver's license, student ID, hostel card, etc.
- ❏ Tickets & confirmations: flights, hotels, trains, rail pass, car rental, sight entries
- ❏ Photocopies of important documents
- ❏ Insurance details
- ❏ Guidebooks & maps
- ❏ Extra passport photos
- ❏ Notepad & pen
- ❏ Journal

Toiletries

- ❏ Soap, shampoo, toothbrush, toothpaste, floss, deodorant, sunscreen, brush/comb, etc.
- ❏ Medicines & vitamins
- ❏ First-aid kit
- ❏ Glasses/contacts/sunglasses
- ❏ Face masks & hand sanitizer
- ❏ Sewing kit
- ❏ Packet of tissues (for WC)
- ❏ Earplugs

Electronics

- ❏ Mobile phone
- ❏ Camera & related gear
- ❏ Tablet/ebook reader/laptop
- ❏ Headphones/earbuds
- ❏ Chargers & batteries
- ❏ Plug adapters

Miscellaneous

- ❏ Daypack
- ❏ Sealable plastic baggies
- ❏ Laundry supplies
- ❏ Small umbrella
- ❏ Travel alarm/watch

Optional Extras

- ❏ Second pair of shoes
- ❏ Travel hairdryer
- ❏ Disinfecting wipes
- ❏ Water bottle
- ❏ Fold-up tote bag
- ❏ Small flashlight & binoculars
- ❏ Small towel or washcloth
- ❏ Tiny lock

Italian Survival Phrases

Hello. (informal)	Ciao.	chow
Good day.	Buongiorno.	bwohn-**jor**-noh
Do you speak English?	Parla inglese?	**par**-lah een-**gleh**-zay
Yes. / No.	Sì. / No.	see / noh
I (don't) understand.	(Non) capisco.	(nohn) kah-**pees**-koh
Please.	Per favore.	pehr fah-**voh**-ray
Thank you.	Grazie.	**graht**-see-ay
You're welcome.	Prego.	**preh**-go
I'm sorry.	Mi dispiace.	mee dee-spee-**ah**-chay
Excuse me.	Mi scusi.	mee **skoo**-zee
No problem.	*Non c'è problema.*	nohn cheh proh-**bleh**-mah
Goodbye.	Arrivederci.	ah-ree-veh-**dehr**-chee
one / two / three	uno / due / tre	**oo**-noh / **doo**-ay / tray
How much is it?	Quanto costa?	**kwahn**-toh **koh**-stah
I'd like / We'd like...	Vorrei / Vorremmo...	voh-**reh**-ee / voh-**reh**-moh
...a room.	...una camera.	**oo**-nah **kah**-meh-rah
...a ticket to _____.	...un biglietto per _____.	oon beel-**yeh**-toh pehr ____
Where is...?	Dov'è...?	doh-**veh**
...the train station	...la stazione	lah staht-see-**oh**-nay
...tourist information	...informazioni turisti	een-for-maht-see-**oh**-nee too-**ree**-stee
...the bathroom	...il bagno	eel **bahn**-yoh
men / women	uomini, signori / donne, signore	**woh**-mee-nee, seen-**yoh**-ree / **doh**-nay, seen-**yoh**-ray
left / right / straight	sinistra / destra / sempre dritto	see-**nee**-strah / **deh**-strah / **sehm**-pray **dree**-toh
What time does this open / close?	A che ora apre / chiude?	ah kay **oh**-rah **ah**-pray / kee-**oo**-day
now / soon / later	adesso / presto / tardi	ah-**deh**-soh / **preh**-stoh / **tar**-dee
today / tomorrow	oggi / domani	**oh**-jee / doh-**mah**-nee

In an Italian Restaurant

I'd like / We'd like...	Vorrei / Vorremmo... voh-**reh**-ee / voh-**reh**-moh
...to reserve a table for one / two.	...prenotare un tavolo per uno / due. preh-noh-**tah**-ray oon **tah**-voh-loh pehr **oo**-noh / **doo**-ay
...the menu (in English).	...il menù (in inglese). eel meh-**noo** (een een-**gleh**-zay)
service (not) included	servizio (non) compreso sehr-**veet**-see-oh (nohn) kohm-**pray**-zoh
cover charge	pane e coperto **pah**-nay ay koh-**pehr**-toh
to go	da portar via dah **por**-tar **vee**-ah
with / without	con / senza kohn / **sehnt**-sah
and / or	e / o ay / oh
breakfast / lunch / dinner	colazione / pranzo / cena koh-laht-zee-**oh**-nay / **prahn**-zoh / **chay**-nah
menu (of the day)	menù (d el giorno) meh-**noo** (dehl **jor**-noh)
specialty of the house	specialità della casa speh-chah-lee-**tah** deh-lah **kah**-zah
sandwich	panino pah-**nee**-noh
soup / salad	zuppa / insalata **tsoo**-pah / een-sah-**lah**-tah
meat / chicken	carne / pollo **kar**-nay / **poh**-loh
fish / seafood	pesce / frutti di mare **peh**-shay / **froo**-tee dee **mah**-ray
fruit / vegetables	frutta / verdure **froo**-tah / vehr-**doo**-ray
dessert	dolce **dohl**-chay
tap water	acqua del rubinetto **ah**-kwah dehl roo-bee-**neh**-toh
coffee / tea	caffè / tè kah-**feh** / teh
wine / beer	vino / birra **vee**-noh / **bee**-rah
red / white	rosso / bianco **roh**-soh / bee-**ahn**-koh
glass / bottle	bicchiere / bottiglia bee-kee-**eh**-ray / boh-**teel**-yah
The bill, please.	Il conto, per favore. eel **kohn**-toh pehr fah-**voh**-ray
Do you accept credit cards?	Accettate carte di credito? ah-cheh-**tah**-tay **kar**-tay dee **kreh**-dee-toh
Delicious!	Delizioso! day-leet-see-**oh**-zoh

For more user-friendly Italian phrases, check out *Rick Steves Italian Phrase Book* or *Rick Steves French, Italian, & German Phrase Book*.

INDEX

A

Accommodations. *See* Sleeping
Aeneas, Anchises, and Ascanius (Bernini): 117
Airports: 200–201
Ancient Rome: 6; eating, 187; history, 37, 43, 53; maps, 128, 193; sightseeing, 126–137; sleeping near, 178
Apollo and Daphne (Bernini): 114–115
Apollo Belvedere: 86–87
Appian Way: 158–159
Apps: 11, 198, 200, 201, 206, 208
Arch of Constantine: 9, 35, 126. *See also* Colosseum; Roman Forum
Arch of Septimius Severus: 51–52. *See also* Roman Forum
Arch of Titus: 43–44. *See also* Roman Forum
Audioguides: 11

B

Baggage, packing: 12–13, 209
Banking: 12. *See also* Money
Basilica Aemilia: 50. *See also* Roman Forum
Basilica of Constantine: 45. *See also* Roman Forum
Basilica S. Maria degli Angeli: 9
Baths of Caracalla: 159–160
Baths of Diocletian: 9, 151–152
Belvedere Torso: 88–89
Bernini, Gian Lorenzo: 113–117, 119–121
Bocca della Verità: 129
Bookstores: 200
Borghese Gallery: 8, 145; general information, 110–111; maps, 111, 120; tour, 109–123
Bruno, Giordano, statue of: 17
Bus tours: 169
Buses: 30, 201, 203; tickets, 202

C

Cabs. *See* Taxis
Caffé Tazza d'Oro: 20–21
Caligula's Palace: 47. *See also* Roman Forum
Campo de' Fiori: 16–17, 142; eating near, 191; map, 195; sleeping near, 181
Canova, Antonio: 112–113
Capitoline Hill: 30, 129–134; map, 130
Capitoline Museums: 8, 131–132
Capuchin Crypt: 145–147
Caravaggio: 107, 118–119
Cars: arrival by, 202; and driver service, 169
Castel Sant'Angelo: 9, 144
Catacombs: 9, 149, 158–159; of Priscilla, 149
Cell phones: 12, 207–208
Cemeteries. *See* Catacombs; Protestant Cemetery
Charlemagne: 64
Churches and cathedrals: Basilica S. Maria degli Angeli, 9; Church of San Clemente, 155–156; Church of San Giovanni in Laterano, 9, 153–154; Church of San Luigi dei Francesi, 141; Church of Santa Maria degli Angeli, 151–152; Church of Santa Maria della Vittoria, 152; Church of Santa Maria in Trastevere, 156; Church of Santa Maria Maggiore, 155; Church of Santa Maria sopra Minerva, 141; Church of Sant'Agnese, 20; Church of Sant'Ignazio, 141; Gesù Church, 141–142; near the Pantheon, 140–142; Santa Maria in Aracoeli Church, 131; St. Paul's Outside the Walls Basilica, 161–162; St. Peter-in-Chains, 8, 137; St. Peter's Basilica, 8, 55–77, 143; tips for visiting, 127
Ciampino Airport: 201

Colosseum: 8, 126, 127; eating near, 187; general information, 26, 30; legacy, 36–38; maps, 28, 31; tour, 25–38

Column of Phocas: 53–54. *See also* Roman Forum

Creation of Adam, The (Michelangelo): 100–101

Credit cards: 199. *See also* Money

Cruise ships: 202

Cuisine: 186. *See also* Eating

Curia, The (Senate House): 50–51. *See also* Roman Forum

Customs: 171

D

Da Vinci, Leonardo: 106

Danäe (Correggio): 122

David (Bernini): 113–114

Debit cards: 199. *See also* Money

Department stores: 170

Deposition (Raphael): 121–122

Dolce Vita Stroll: 8–9, 147

E

East Rome: 7; sightseeing, 149–156

Eating: cuisine, 186; general information, 183–184; language, 212; listings, 187–192; maps, 193–196; price code, 184; quick budget meals, 185–186; restaurants, 184–185; tipping, 207

Egyptian art, in the Vatican Museums: 84–86

Electricity: 198

Emergencies: 199

Entertainment: 172–174

E.U.R.: 162

F

Fiumicino Airport: 200–201

Food. *See* Eating

Forum. *See* Roman Forum

Four Rivers Fountain: 17–20

Francis I, Pope: 69

G

Galleria Doria Pamphilj: 142

Garden of Eden, The (Michelangelo): 101

Gesù Church: 141–142

Goat Amalthea with the Child Jupiter and a Faun, The (Bernini): 121

H

Hadrian's Villa: 164–165

History of Rome: 37, 43, 53

Holy Stairs: 153–154

Hotels: 176. *See also* Sleeping

House of the Vestal Virgins: 46–47. *See also* Roman Forum

I

Imperial Forums: 135–137

Italian survival phrases: 211

Itineraries: 10

J

Jazz music: 172

Jewish Quarter: 134–135

John Paul II, Pope: 75

John XXIII, Pope: 70

L

Language: 211–212

Laocoön: 87–88

Last Judgment, The (Michelangelo): 102–105

Laundry: 200

Leonardo da Vinci Airport: 200–201

Liberation of St. Peter, The (Raphael): 94

Local guides: 168

Luggage, packing: 12–13, 209

M

Mamertine Prison: 9, 132

Markets: 171

Mausoleum of Augustus: 148–149

Medical help: 199

Metro: 203; map, 204–205; tickets, 202

Michelangelo: in the Sistine Chapel (Vatican Museums), 97–105; in St. Peter's Basilica, 64–65, 73–75
Mobile phones: 12, 207–208
Money: 206; banking, 12; credit and debit cards, 199; tipping, 207
Monte Palatino. *See* Palatine Hill
Monte Testaccio: 160
Montemartini Museum: 161
Monti neighborhood: 137; eating, 187; nightlife, 174
Mouth of Truth: 129
Movies: 173
Mummies, in the Vatican Museums: 84
Museo dell'Ara Pacis: 8, 148
Museums: Borghese Gallery, 8, 109–123, 145; Capitoline Museums, 8, 131–132; Castel Sant'Angelo, 9, 144; Galleria Doria Pamphilj, 142; Mamertine Prison, 9, 132; Montemartini Museum, 161; Museo dell'Ara Pacis, 8, 148; Museum of the Imperial Forums, 136; National Museum of Rome, 8, 149–150; Treasury Museum (St. Peter's Basilica), 75; Vatican Museums, 8, 79–107, 143–144
Music: 172

N
National Museum of Rome: 8, 149–150
Neighborhoods: 6–10; map, 7; shopping, 170. *See also specific neighborhoods*
Nightlife: 172–174
North Rome: 7; maps, 146; nightlife, 174; sightseeing, 145–149

O
Opera: 172
Ostia Antica: 162–163

P
Packing: 12–13; checklist, 209
Palace of Tiberius: 47. *See also* Roman Forum
Palantine Hill: 127, 128–129
Palatine Hill: 9
Palazzo Valentini, The Roman House at: 9, 136–137
Pantheon: 8, 20, 138–140; eating near, 189–190; map, 194; sleeping near, 180
Pantheon neighborhood: 6–7; churches near the Pantheon, 140–142; eating near, 189–191; maps, 139, 194; sightseeing, 138–142; sleeping, 180–181
Passports: 11, 199
Paul V, Pope, bust of: 121
Pauline Borghese as Venus (Canova): 112–113
Peak season: 10
Pharmacies: 200
Phones: 12, 207–208
Piazza Capranica: 21
Piazza Colonna: 22
Piazza del Campidoglio: 9, 131
Piazza di Montecitorio: 21
Piazza Navona: 17–20, 142; eating near, 189
Piazza Venezia: 133; map, 130
Pickpockets: 13, 199
Picnicking: 127
Pietà (Michelangelo): 73–75
Pilgrim's Rome: 152–156; map, 154
Pinacoteca (Vatican Museums): 106–107
Planning: general information, 11–13; itineraries, 10; when to go, 10–11
Popes: seeing the pope, 57; succession, 66. *See also specific popes*
Porta San Paolo: 160
Protestant Cemetery: 160
Pyramid of Gaius: 160

R
Rape of Proserpina, The (Bernini): 115–117
Raphael: 94; in the Borghese Gallery,

121–122; in the Vatican Museums, 92–96, 106

Renaissance art, in the Vatican Museums: 92–96

Restaurants: 184–185; language, 212; tipping, 207. *See also* Eating

Rick Steves Audio Europe: 11

Rick Steves Classroom Europe: 11

RickSteves.com: 208

Roma Pass: 127

Roman Forum: 8, 126, 127; general information, 40; map, 41; tour, 37–54

Roman House at Palazzo Valentini: 9, 136–137

Rome: city maps, 4–5, 7, 18–19; history, 37, 43, 53

Rostrum: 51. *See also* Roman Forum

S

Sacred and Profane Love (Titian): 122–123

Safety: 199

Santa Maria in Aracoeli Church: 131

School of Athens, The (Raphael): 94–96

Shopping: department stores, 170; hours, 170; neighborhoods, 170; street markets, 171; VAT and customs, 171

Sightseeing: Ancient Rome, 126–137; East Rome, 149–156; near Rome, 162–165; North Rome, 145–149; Pantheon neighborhood, 138–142; South Rome, 157–162; tips, 127, 198; Trastevere, 156–157; Vatican City, 142–144. *See also specific sights*

Sistine Chapel (Vatican Museums): 97–105

Sleeping: budget tips, 177; general information, 175; hotels, 176; listings, 178–182; making reservations, 176; price code, 177

Smartphones: 12, 207–208

Soccer: 174

Sound-and-light shows: 173

South Rome: 10; sightseeing, 157–162

Spanish Steps: 23–24, 147; eating near, 190; map, 194

St. Paul's Outside the Walls Basilica: 161–162

St. Peter: 67–70, 73

St. Peter-in-Chains Church: 8, 137

St. Peter's Basilica: 8, 143; general information, 56–57; maps, 59, 63; tour, 55–77. *See also* Vatican City

St. Peter's Square: 58–61

Subway. *See* Metro

T

Taxis: 30, 200–201, 203–206; tipping, 207

Temple of Antoninus Pius and Faustina: 46. *See also* Roman Forum

Temple of Castor and Pollux: 48. *See also* Roman Forum

Temple of Julius Caesar: 49–50. *See also* Roman Forum

Temple of Saturn: 52. *See also* Roman Forum

Temple of Venus: 35–36. *See also* Colosseum

Temple of Vesta: 46. *See also* Roman Forum

Termini Station: 201; eating near, 188; maps, 151, 193; sightseeing nearby, 149–152; sleeping near, 178–180. *See also* Trains

Testaccio: 160–162; map, 161; nightlife, 174

Theft: 13, 199

Tiburtina Station: 202

Time zones: 198

Titian: 122–123

Tivoli: 163–165

Tourist information: 30, 198

Tours: 168–169

Trains: 200, 201–202

Trajan's Column, Market, and Forum: 8, 135–136

Transportation: around Rome, 202–206; to and from Rome, 200–202; tickets, 202

Trastevere: 10; eating near, 191–192; map, 195; nightlife, 174; sightseeing, 156–157; sleeping, 181

Travel advisories: 198

Travel insurance: 12

Treasury Museum (St. Peter's Basilica): 75

Trevi Fountain: 9, 22–23, 142

U

Uber: 206

V

VAT refunds: 171

Vatican City: 7, 76; eating near, 192; maps, 143, 196; sightseeing, 142–144; sleeping near, 182; tours, 57. See also St. Peter's Basilica

Vatican Museums: 8, 143–144; general information, 80–81; maps, 82, 83, 85, 90, 93; tour, 79–107

Via del Corso: 22

Via Sacra: 45. See also Roman Forum

Victor Emmanuel Monument: 9, 133–134

Villa Borghese Gardens: 145

Villa de'Este: 163–165

Villa Farnesina: 156–157

W

Walking tours companies: 168

Walking tours, self-guided: Colosseum, 25–38; heart of Rome, 15–24; Roman Forum, 37–54

WCs: 30

Websites, helpful: 199

Wi-Fi: 207–208

Winter season: 10–11

Start your trip at

Our website enhances this book and turns

Explore Europe

At ricksteves.com you can browse through thousands of articles, videos, photos and radio interviews, plus find a wealth of money-saving travel tips for planning your dream trip. And with our mobile-friendly website, you can easily access all this great travel information anywhere you go.

TV Shows

Preview the places you'll visit by watching entire half-hour episodes of *Rick Steves' Europe* (choose from all 100 shows) on-demand, for free.

ricksteves.com

your travel dreams into affordable reality

Radio Interviews

Enjoy ready access to Rick's vast library of radio interviews covering travel tips and cultural insights that relate specifically to your Europe travel plans.

Travel Forums

Learn, ask, share! Our online community of savvy travelers is a great resource for first-time travelers to Europe, as well as seasoned pros.

Travel News

Subscribe to our free Travel News e-newsletter, and get monthly updates from Rick on what's happening in Europe.

Classroom Europe®

Check out our free resource for educators with 500 short video clips from the *Rick Steves' Europe* TV show.

Audio Europe™

Rick's Free Travel App

Get your FREE Rick Steves Audio Europe™ app to enjoy…

- Dozens of self-guided tours of Europe's top museums, sights and historic walks
- Hundreds of tracks filled with cultural insights and sightseeing tips from Rick's radio interviews
- All organized into handy geographic playlists
- For Apple and Android

With Rick whispering in your ear, Europe gets even better.

Find out more at ricksteves.com

Pack Light and Right

Gear up for your next adventure at ricksteves.com

Light Luggage

Pack light and right with Rick Steves' affordable, custom-designed rolling carry-on bags, backpacks, day packs and shoulder bags.

Accessories

From packing cubes to moneybelts and beyond, Rick has personally selected the travel goodies that will help your trip go smoother.

Shop at ricksteves.com

Rick Steves has

Experience maximum Europe

Save time and energy

This guidebook is your independent-travel toolkit. But for all it delivers, it's still up to you to devote the time and energy it takes to manage the preparation and logistics that are essential for a happy trip. If that's a hassle, there's a solution.

Rick Steves Tours

A Rick Steves tour takes you to Europe's most interesting places with great guides and small groups.

great tours, too!

with minimum stress

We follow Rick's favorite itineraries, ride in comfy buses, stay in family-run hotels, and bring you intimately close to the Europe you've traveled so far to see. Most importantly, we take away the logistical headaches so you can focus on the fun.

Join the fun

This year we'll take thousands of free-spirited travelers—nearly half of them repeat customers—along with us on four dozen different itineraries, from Ireland to Italy to Athens. Is a Rick Steves tour the right fit for your travel dreams? Find out at ricksteves.com, where you can check seat availability and sign up.

Europe is best experienced with happy travel partners. We hope you can join us.

See our itineraries at ricksteves.com

A Guide for Every Trip

BEST OF GUIDES

Full-color guides in an easy-to-scan format, focusing on top sights and experiences in popular destinations

Best of England
Best of Europe
Best of France
Best of Germany

Best of Ireland
Best of Italy
Best of Scotland
Best of Spain

COMPREHENSIVE GUIDES

City, country, and regional guides printed on Bible-thin paper. Packed with detailed coverage for a multi-week trip exploring iconic sights and more

Amsterdam &
  the Netherlands
Barcelona
Belgium: Bruges, Brussels,
  Antwerp & Ghent
Berlin
Budapest
Central Europe
Croatia & Slovenia
England
Florence & Tuscany
France
Germany
Great Britain
Greece: Athens &
  the Peloponnese
Iceland

Ireland
Istanbul
Italy
London
Paris
Portugal
Prague & the Czech Republi
Provence & the French
  Riviera
Rome
Scandinavia
Scotland
Sicily
Spain
Switzerland
Venice
Vienna, Salzburg & Tirol

Many guides are available as ebooks.

POCKET GUIDES
Compact guides for shorter city trips

Amsterdam
Athens
Barcelona
Florence

Italy's Cinque Terre
London
Munich & Salzburg
Paris

Prague
Rome
Venice
Vienna

SNAPSHOT GUIDES
Focused single-destination coverage

Basque Country: Spain & France
Copenhagen & the Best of Denmark
Dublin
Dubrovnik
Edinburgh
Hill Towns of Central Italy
Krakow, Warsaw & Gdansk
Lisbon
Loire Valley
Madrid & Toledo
Milan & the Italian Lakes District
Naples & the Amalfi Coast
Nice & the French Riviera
Normandy
Northern Ireland
Norway
Reykjavík
Rothenburg & the Rhine
Sevilla, Granada & Southern Spain
St. Petersburg, Helsinki & Tallinn
Stockholm

CRUISE PORTS GUIDES
Reference for cruise ports of call

Mediterranean Cruise Ports
Scandinavian & Northern European
  Cruise Ports

TRAVEL SKILLS & CULTURE
Greater information and insight

Europe 101
Europe Through the Back Door
Europe's Top 100 Masterpieces
European Christmas
European Easter
European Festivals
For the Love of Europe
Italy for Food Lovers
Travel as a Political Act

PHRASE BOOKS & DICTIONARIES

French
French, Italian & German
German
Italian
Portuguese
Spanish

PLANNING MAPS

Britain, Ireland & London
Europe
France & Paris
Germany, Austria & Switzerland
Iceland
Ireland
Italy
Portugal
Scotland
Spain & Portugal

PHOTO CREDITS

Avalon Travel
Hachette Book Group
City Center
555 12 Street, 18th Floor
Oakland, CA 94607

Printed in Malaysia for Imago
Fifth Edition
Second printing June 2024

ISBN 978-1-64171-545-4

For the latest on Rick's talks, guidebooks, tours, public television series, and public radio show, contact Rick Steves' Europe, 130 Fourth Avenue North, Edmonds, WA 98020, +1 425 771 8303, RickSteves.com, rick@ricksteves.com.

Rick Steves' Europe
Managing Editor: Jennifer Madison Davis
Assistant Managing Editor: Cathy Lu
Editors: Glenn Eriksen, Suzanne Kotz, Rosie Leutzinger, Teresa Nemeth, Jessica Shaw, Carrie Shepherd
Editorial & Production Assistant: Megan Simms
Graphic Content Director: Sandra Hundacker
Maps & Graphics: Orin Dubrow, David C. Hoerlein, Lauren Mills, Mary Rostad, Laura Terrenzio

Avalon Travel
Senior Editor and Series Manager: Madhu Prasher
Associate Managing Editor: Jamie Andrade
Editor: Sierra Machado
Copy Editor: Kelly Lydick
Proofreader: Maggie Ryan
Indexer: Claire Splan
Production & Typesetting: Christine DeLorenzo, Rue Flaherty, Jane Musser
Cover Design: Kimberly Glyder Design
Interior Design: Darren Alessi
Maps & Graphics: Kat Bennett

Let's Keep on Travelin'

Your trip doesn't need to end.

Follow Rick on social media!

Rick Steves POCKET

ROME

Including maps of Rome, South Rome,
the Colosseum, St. Peter's Basilica, Roman Forum,
Heart of Rome Walk, and Rome Transportation

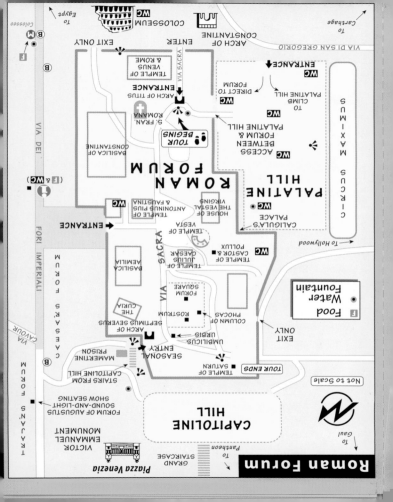

Roman Forum

Not to Scale

To Gaul

CAPITOLINE HILL

Piazza Venezia

To Pantheon

GRAND STAIRCASE

VICTOR EMMANUEL MONUMENT

FORUM OF AUGUSTUS

SOUND-AND-LIGHT SHOW SEATING

TRAJAN'S FORUM

CAESAR'S FORUM

MAMERTINE PRISON

STAIRS FROM CAPITOLINE HILL

SEASONAL ENTRY

TEMPLE OF SATURN

TOUR ENDS

ARCH OF SEPTIMIUS SEVERUS

THE CURIA

UMBILICUS URBIS

COLUMN OF PHOCAS

ROSTRUM

BASILICA AEMILIA

FORUM SQUARE

VIA SACRA

Food Water Fountain

EXIT ONLY

TEMPLE OF CASTOR & POLLUX

TEMPLE OF JULIUS CAESAR

TEMPLE OF VESTA

HOUSE OF THE VESTAL VIRGINS

TEMPLE OF ANTONINUS PIUS & FAUSTINA

WC

ENTRANCE

ROMAN FORUM

BASILICA OF CONSTANTINE

PALATINE HILL

CALIGULA'S PALACE

ACCESS BETWEEN FORUM & PALATINE HILL

WC

WC

WC

To Hollywood

CIRCUS MAXIMUS

TO CLIMB PALATINE HILL

DIRECT TO FORUM

ENTRANCE

WC

WC

S. FRAN. ROMANA

TOUR BEGINS

ARCH OF TITUS

ENTRANCE

TEMPLE OF VENUS & ROME

EXIT ONLY

ENTER

COLOSSEUM

WC

ARCH OF CONSTANTINE

VIA DI SAN GREGORIO

To Carthage

To Egypt

Colosseo

B M

E

B

VIA DEI

(E & WC)

FORI IMPERIALI

VIA CAVOUR